Fremdsprachentexte

Roald Dahl
Three Tales of the Unexpected

William and Mary
The Wish
Pig

Herausgegeben von
Harald Beck

Philipp Reclam jun. Stuttgart

Diese Ausgabe darf nur in der Bundesrepublik Deutschland, in Österreich und in der Schweiz vertrieben werden. Die englischen Texte folgen den Ausgaben: Roald Dahl, *Kiss Kiss*, Harmondsworth: Penguin Books, 1962 (*William and Mary, Pig*), und: Roald Dahl, *Someone Like You*, Harmondsworth: Penguin Books, 1970 (*The Wish*).

Universal-Bibliothek Nr. 9215

Abdruck mit Genehmigung von Mohrbooks, Zürich
Gesamtherstellung: Reclam, Ditzingen. Printed in Germany 1993

ISBN 3-15-009215-9

William and Mary

William Pearl did not leave a great deal of money when he died, and his will was a simple one. With the exception of a few small bequests to relatives, he left all his property to his wife.

The solicitor and Mrs Pearl went over it together in the solicitor's office, and when the business was completed, the widow got up to leave. At that point, the solicitor took a sealed envelope from the folder on his desk and held it out to his client.

"I have been instructed to give you this," he said. "Your husband sent it to us shortly before he passed away." The solicitor was pale and prim, and out of respect for a widow he kept his head on one side as he spoke, looking downward. "It appears that it might be something personal, Mrs Pearl. No doubt you'd like to take it home with you and read it in privacy."

3 **will:** Testament.
4 **bequest:** Erbe, Legat.
relative: Verwandte(r).
4f. **property:** Besitz, Vermögen.
6 **solicitor:** Anwalt.
to go over s.th.: etwas dụrchgehen, durchsehen.
9 **sealed:** versiegelt.
folder: Mappe, Aktendeckel.
10 **client:** Klient(in).
12 **to pass away:** versterben, verscheiden.
13 **prim:** steif, formell.
17 **in privacy:** ungestört, in Ruhe.

Mrs Pearl accepted the envelope and went out into the street. She paused on the pavement, feeling the thing with her fingers. A letter of farewell from William? Probably, yes. A formal letter. It was bound to be formal – stiff and formal. The man was incapable of acting otherwise. He had never done anything informal in his life.

> My dear Mary, I trust that you will not permit my departure from this world to upset you too much, but that you will continue to observe those precepts which have guided you so well during our partnership together. Be diligent and dignified in all things. Be thrifty with your money. Be very careful that you do not . . . et cetera, et cetera.

A typical William letter.

Or was it possible that he might have broken down at the last moment and written her something beautiful? Maybe this was a beautiful tender message, a sort of love letter, a lovely warm note of thanks to her for giving him thirty years of her life and for ironing a million shirts and cooking a million meals and making a million beds, something that she could read over and over again, once

4 **formal:** förmlich, feierlich, formell.
to be bound to: müssen.
5 **incapable:** unfähig, nicht imstande.
8 **to trust:** hoffen, zuversichtlich sein, glauben.
departure: hier: Weggang.
9 **to upset:** aus der Fassung bringen, aufregen.
10 **to observe:** befolgen, be(ob)achten.
precept: Gebot, Regel, Grundsatz.
11 **partnership:** Partnerschaft.
diligent: fleißig, emsig.
dignified: würdevoll, würdig.
12 **thrifty:** sparsam, haushälterisch.
18 **warm:** herzlich.

a day at least, and she would keep it for ever in the box on the dressing-table together with her brooches.

There is no knowing what people will do when they are about to die, Mrs Pearl told herself, and she tucked the envelope under her arm and hurried home.

She let herself in the front door and went straight to the living-room and sat down on the sofa without removing her hat or coat. Then she opened the envelope and drew out the contents. These consisted, she saw, of some fifteen or twenty sheets of lined white paper, folded over once and held together at the top left-hand corner by a clip. Each sheet was covered with the small, neat, forward-sloping writing that she knew so well, but when she noticed how much of it there was, and in what a neat businesslike manner it was written, and how the first page didn't even begin in the nice way a letter should, she began to get suspicious.

She looked away. She lit herself a cigarette. She took one puff and laid the cigarette in the ash-tray.

If this is about what I am beginning to suspect it is about, she told herself, then I don't want to read it.

2 **dressing-table:** Toilettentisch.
brooch: Brosche, Spange.
4 **to tuck:** (weg)stecken, klemmen.
7 **to remove:** (ein Kleidungsstück) abnehmen, ablegen.
10 **lined:** liniert.
12 **clip:** (Büro-)Klammer.
neat: sauber, ordentlich.
12 f. **forward-sloping:** rechtsschräg, vorwärts geneigt.
15 **businesslike:** geschäftsmäßig, sachlich, nüchtern.
17 **suspicious:** mißtrauisch, argwöhnisch.
18 f. **to take a puff:** einen Zug machen, (an einer Zigarette) ziehen.
19 **ash-tray:** Aschenbecher.
20 **to suspect:** vermuten, befürchten.

Can one refuse to read a letter from the dead?
Yes.
Well . . .
She glanced over at William's empty chair on the other side of the fireplace. It was a big brown leather armchair, and there was a depression on the seat of it, made by his buttocks over the years. Higher up, on the backrest, there was a dark oval stain on the leather where his head had rested. He used to sit reading in that chair and she would be opposite him on the sofa, sewing on buttons or mending socks or putting a patch on the elbow of one of his jackets, and every now and then a pair of eyes would glance up from the book and settle on her, watchful, but strangely impersonal, as if calculating something. She had never liked those eyes. They were ice blue, cold, small, and rather close together, with two deep vertical lines of disapproval dividing them. All her life they had been watching her. And even now, after a week alone in the house, she sometimes had an uneasy feeling that they were still there, following her around, staring at her from doorways, from empty chairs, through a window at night.
Slowly she reached into her handbag and took out her spectacles and put them on. Then, holding the pages up high in front of her so that they caught the late afternoon light from the window behind, she started to read:

5 **armchair:** Lehnstuhl, Sessel.
6 **depression:** Vertiefung.
7 **buttocks** (pl.): Hintern, Gesäß.
backrest: Rückenstütze, -lehne.
14 **impersonal:** unpersönlich.
16 **vertical:** senkrecht.
17 **disapproval:** Mißbilligung, Tadel.

This note, my dear Mary, is entirely for you, and will be given you shortly after I am gone.

Do not be alarmed by the sight of all this writing. It is nothing but an attempt on my part to explain to you precisely what Landy is going to do to me, and why I have agreed that he should do it, and what are his theories and his hopes. You are my wife and you have a right to know these things. In fact you *must* know them. During the past few days I have tried very hard to speak with you about Landy, but you have steadfastly refused to give me a hearing. This, as I have already told you, is a very foolish attitude to take, and I find it not entirely an unselfish one either. It stems mostly from ignorance, and I am absolutely convinced that if only you were made aware of all the facts, you would immediately change your view. That is why I am hoping that when I am no longer with you, and your mind is less distracted, you will consent to listen to me more carefully through these pages. I swear to you that when you have read my story, your sense of antipathy will vanish, and enthusiasm will take its place. I even dare to hope that you will become a little proud of what I have done.

As you read on, you must forgive me, if you will, for the coolness of my style, but this is the only way I know of getting my message over to you clearly. You see, as my time draws near, it is natural that I begin to brim with

3 **to alarm:** beunruhigen, erschrecken.
10 **steadfastly** (adv.): beharrlich, beständig.
13 **unselfish:** selbstlos, uneigennützig.
to stem from s.th.: von etwas abstammen, auf etwas zurückgehen.
17 **distracted:** verwirrt, heftig erregt.
20 **antipathy:** Abneigung, Widerwille.
26 **to brim:** (bis zum Rand) voll sein, strotzen.

every kind of sentimentality under the sun. Each day I grow more extravagantly wistful, especially in the evenings, and unless I watch myself closely my emotions will be overflowing on to these pages.

I have a wish, for example, to write something about you and what a satisfactory wife you have been to me through the years, and I am promising myself that if there is time, and I still have the strength, I shall do that next.

I have a yearning also to speak about this Oxford of mine where I have been living and teaching for the past seventeen years, to tell something about the glory of the place and to explain, if I can, a little of what it has meant to have been allowed to work in its midst. All the things and places that I loved so well keep crowding in on me now in this gloomy bedroom. They are bright and beautiful as they always were, and today, for some reason, I can see them more clearly than ever. The path around the lake in the gardens of Worcester College, where Lovelace used to walk. The gateway at Pembroke. The view westward over the town from Magdalen Tower. The great hall at Christchurch. The little rockery at St John's where I have counted more than a dozen varieties of campanula, including the rare and dainty C. Waldsteiniana. But there, you see! I haven't even begun and already I'm

2 **extravagantly** (adv.): übermäßig, übertrieben.
wistful: ernst, melancholisch, nachdenklich.
9 **yearning:** Verlangen.
15 **gloomy:** düster, trübsinnig.
18 **Lovelace:** Richard L. (1618–58), englischer Dichter der sogenannten Cavalier School, Hofmann und Gelehrter; studierte in Oxford.
19 **gateway:** Tor(gang).
21 **rockery:** Steingarten, Alpinum.
22 **campanula:** Glockenblume.
23 **dainty:** zierlich, exquisit.

falling into the trap. So let me get started now; and let you read it slowly, my dear, without any of that sense of sorrow or disapproval that might otherwise embarrass your understanding. Promise me now that you will read it slowly, and that you will put yourself in a cool and patient frame of mind before you begin.

The details of the illness that struck me down so suddenly in my middle life are known to you. I need not waste time upon them – except to admit at once how foolish I was not to have gone earlier to my doctor. Cancer is one of the few remaining diseases that these modern drugs cannot cure. A surgeon can operate if it has not spread too far; but with me, not only did I leave it too late, but the thing had the effrontery to attack me in the pancreas, making both surgery and survival equally impossible.

So here I was with somewhere between one and six months left to live, growing more melancholy every hour – and then, all of a sudden, in comes Landy.

That was six weeks ago, on a Tuesday morning, very early, long before your visiting time, and the moment he entered I knew there was some sort of madness in the wind. He didn't creep in on his toes, sheepish and embarrassed, not knowing what to say, like all my other vis-

3 **to embarrass:** hier: erschweren, behindern.
6 **frame of mind:** Gemütszustand, Stimmung.
10 **cancer:** Krebs (Krankheit).
11 **drug:** (Arznei-)Mittel, Medikament.
12 **surgeon:** Chirurg.
14 **effrontery:** Frechheit, Unverfrorenheit.
pancreas: Bauchspeicheldrüse.
15 **surgery:** (operativer) Eingriff.
21f. **to be in the wind:** (fig.) in der Luft liegen.
22 **sheepish:** ängstlich; hilflos; belämmert.

itors. He came in strong and smiling, and he strode up to the bed and stood there looking down at me with a wild bright glimmer in his eyes, and he said, "William, my boy, this is perfect. You're just the one I want!"

Perhaps I should explain to you here that although John Landy has never been to our house, and you have seldom if ever met him, I myself have been friendly with him for at least nine years. I am, of course, primarily a teacher of philosophy, but as you know I've lately been dabbling a good deal in psychology as well. Landy's interests and mine have therefore slightly overlapped. He is a magnificent neuro-surgeon, one of the finest, and recently he has been kind enough to let me study the results of some of his work, especially the varying effects of prefrontal lobotomies upon different types of psychopath. So you can see that when he suddenly burst in on me that Tuesday morning, we were by no means strangers to one another.

"Look," he said, pulling up a chair beside the bed. "In a few weeks you're going to be dead. Correct?"

Coming from Landy, the question didn't seem especially unkind. In a way it was refreshing to have a visitor brave enough to touch upon the forbidden subject.

1 **to stride:** schreiten, große Schritte machen.
3 **glimmer:** Schimmer, Flackern.
8 **primarily** (adv.): in erster Linie, vor allem.
9f. **to dabble in s.th.:** sich aus Liebhaberei mit etwas beschäftigen.
11 **to overlap:** sich überschneiden, sich teilweise decken.
12 **neuro-surgeon:** Neurochirurg.
14 **prefrontal:** präfrontal, auf der vorderen Stirnseite gelegen.
15 **lobotomy:** Lobotomie (operativer Eingriff bei bestimmten Geisteskrankheiten).
psychopath: Psychopath (jd., der an einer abnormen psychischen Verfassung leidet).
23 **forbidden:** verboten, tabu.

"You're going to expire right here in this room, and then they'll take you out and cremate you."

"Bury me," I said.

"That's even worse. And then what? Do you believe you'll go to heaven?"

"I doubt it," I said, "though it would be comforting to think so."

"Or hell, perhaps?"

"I don't really see why they should send me there."

"You never know, my dear William."

"What's all this about?" I asked.

"Well," he said, and I could see him watching me carefully, "personally, I don't believe that after you're dead you'll ever hear of yourself again – unless . . ." and here he paused and smiled and leaned closer ". . . unless, of course, you have the sense to put yourself into my hands. Would you care to consider a proposition?"

The way he was staring at me, and studying me, and appraising me with a queer kind of hungriness, I might have been a piece of prime beef on the counter and he had bought it and was waiting for them to wrap it up.

"I'm really serious about it, William. Would you care to consider a proposition?"

"I don't know what you're talking about."

"Then listen and I'll tell you. Will you listen to me?"

"Go on then, if you like. I doubt I've got very much to lose by hearing it."

1 **to expire:** sterben, verscheiden.
2 **to cremate:** einäschern.
6 **comforting:** tröstlich.
17 **proposition:** Vorschlag.
19 **to appraise:** abschätzen, taxieren.
20 **prime:** erstklassig, vorzüglich.
counter: Ladentisch.

"On the contrary, you have a great deal to gain – especially *after you're dead.*"

I am sure he was expecting me to jump when he said this, but for some reason I was ready for it. I lay quite still, watching his face and that slow white smile of his that always revealed the gold clasp of an upper denture curled around the canine on the left side of his mouth.

"This is a thing, William, that I've been working on quietly for some years. One or two others here at the hospital have been helping me, especially Morrison, and we've completed a number of fairly successful trials with laboratory animals. I'm at the stage now where I'm ready to have a go with a man. It's a big idea, and it may sound a bit far-fetched at first, but from a surgical point of view there doesn't seem to be any reason why it shouldn't be more or less practicable."

Landy leaned forward and placed both hands on the edge of my bed. He has a good face, handsome in a bony sort of way, with none of the usual doctor's look about it. You know that look, most of them have it. It glimmers at you out of their eyeballs like a dull electric sign and it reads *Only I can save you*. But John Landy's eyes were wide

6 **to reveal:** zeigen, sichtbar werden lassen.
clasp: Spange, Klammer.
denture: Gebiß.
7 **canine:** Eckzahn.
12 **laboratory:** Labor.
13 **to have a go** (coll.): (etwas) probieren, versuchen.
14 **far-fetched:** weit hergeholt, ausgefallen.
surgical: chirurgisch.
16 **practicable:** machbar, möglich.
20 **to glimmer:** schimmern.
21 **eyeball:** Augapfel.

and bright and little sparks of excitement were dancing in the centres of them.

"Quite a long time ago," he said, "I saw a short medical film that had been brought over from Russia. It was a rather gruesome thing, but interesting. It showed a dog's head completely severed from the body, but with the normal blood supply being maintained through the arteries and veins by means of an artificial heart. Now the thing is this: that dog's head, sitting there all alone on a sort of tray, was *alive*. The brain was functioning. They proved it by several tests. For example, when food was smeared on the dog's lips, the tongue would come out and lick it away; and the eyes would follow a person moving across the room.

It seemed reasonable to conclude from this that the head and the brain did not need to be attached to the rest of the body in order to remain alive – provided, of course, that a supply of properly oxygenated blood could be maintained.

Now then. My own thought, which grew out of seeing this film, was to remove the brain from the skull of a human and keep it alive and functioning as an independent unit for an unlimited period after he is dead. *Your* brain, for example, after *you* are dead."

5 **gruesome:** grausig; abstoßend.
6 **to sever:** abtrennen, lösen.
7 **supply:** Zufuhr.
8 **artery:** Arterie.
10 **tray:** flache Schale, Tablett.
12 **to smear:** schmieren.
18 **oxygenated:** mit Sauerstoff angereichert (*oxygen:* Sauerstoff).
21 **skull:** Schädel; Hirnschale.
23 **unit:** Einheit.

"I don't like that," I said.

"Don't interrupt, William. Let me finish. So far as I can tell from subsequent experiments, the brain is a peculiarly self-supporting object. It manufactures its own cerebrospinal fluid. The magic processes of thought and memory which go on inside it are manifestly not impaired by the absence of limbs or trunk or even of skull, provided, as I say, that you keep pumping in the right kind of oxygenated blood under the proper conditions.

My dear William, just think for a moment of your own brain. It is in perfect shape. It is crammed full of a lifetime of learning. It has taken you years of work to make it what it is. It is just beginning to give out some first-rate original ideas. Yet soon it is going to have to die along with the rest of your body simply because your silly little pancreas is riddled with cancer."

"No thank you," I said to him. "You can stop there. It's a repulsive idea, and even if you could do it, which I doubt, it would be quite pointless. What possible use is there in keeping my brain alive if I couldn't talk or see or hear or feel? Personally, I can think of nothing more unpleasant."

"I believe that you *would* be able to communicate with us," Landy said. "And we might even succeed in giving

3 **subsequent:** (nach)folgend, später.
4 **self-supporting:** sich selbst versorgend, autark.
5 **cerebrospinal fluid:** Hirnrückenmarksflüssigkeit.
6 **manifestly** (adv.): offenbar; erkennbar.
to be impaired: beeinträchtigt werden.
7 **trunk:** Rumpf, Leib.
11 **crammed:** vollgestopft.
14 **first-rate:** erstklassig, ausgezeichnet.
16 **riddled:** zerfressen, zerstört.
18 **repulsive:** abstoßend, widerwärtig.

you a certain amount of vision. But let's take this slowly. I'll come to all that later on. The fact remains that you're going to die fairly soon whatever happens; and my plans would not involve touching you at all until *after* you are dead. Come now, William. No true philosopher could object to lending his dead body to the cause of science."

"That's not putting it quite straight," I answered. "It seems to me there'd be some doubts as to whether I were dead or alive by the time you'd finished with me."

"Well," he said, smiling a little, "I suppose you're right about that. But I don't think you ought to turn me down quite so quickly, before you know a bit more about it."

"I said I don't want to hear it."

"Have a cigarette," he said, holding out his case.

"I don't smoke, you know that."

He took one himself and lit it with a tiny silver lighter that was no bigger than a shilling piece. "A present from the people who make my instruments," he said. "Ingenious, isn't it?"

I examined the lighter, then handed it back.

"May I go on?" he asked.

"I'd rather you didn't."

"Just lie still and listen. I think you'll find it quite interesting."

There were some blue grapes on a plate beside my bed. I put the plate on my chest and began eating the grapes.

1 **vision:** Sehvermögen.
6 **cause:** (gute) Sache.
8 **straight:** hier: ehrlich, korrekt.
12 **to turn down** (coll.): ablehnen, zurückweisen.
17 **lighter:** Feuerzeug.
19 **ingenious:** klug erdacht, clever.

"At the very moment of death," Landy said, "I should have to be standing by so that I could step in immediately and try to keep your brain alive."

"You mean leaving it in the head?"

"To start with, yes. I'd have to."

"And where would you put it after that?"

"If you want to know, in a sort of basin."

"Are you really serious about this?"

"Certainly I'm serious."

"All right. Go on."

"I suppose you know that when the heart stops and the brain is deprived of fresh blood and oxygen, its tissues die very rapidly. Anything from four to six minutes and the whole thing's dead. Even after three minutes you may get a certain amount of damage. So I should have to work rapidly to prevent this from happening. But with the help of the machine, it should all be quite simple."

"What machine?"

"The artificial heart. We've got a nice adaptation here of the one originally devised by Alexis Carrel and Lindbergh. It oxygenates the blood, keeps it at the right temperature, pumps it in at the right pressure, and does a number of other little necessary things. It's really not at all complicated."

2 **to stand by:** sich bereit halten.
7 **basin:** Schale, Becken.
12 **to deprive:** berauben, entziehen.
tissue: Gewebe.
19 **adaptation:** nachgebautes Modell.
20 **to devise:** erdenken, erfinden.
20/20 f. **Carrel / Lindbergh:** Der französische Chirurg und Physiologe Alexis C. (1873–1944) und Charles A. Lindbergh (1902–72) entwickelten gemeinsam die nach ihnen benannte Pumpapparatur. Ihre Forschungsergebnisse veröffentlichten sie unter dem Titel *The Culture of Organs* (1938).

"Tell me what you would do at the moment of death," I said. "What is the first thing you would do?"

"Do you know anything about the vascular and venous arrangement of the brain?"

"No."

"Then listen. It's not difficult. The blood supply to the brain is derived from two main sources, the internal carotid arteries and the vertebral arteries. There are two of each, making four arteries in all. Got that?"

"Yes."

"And the return system is even simpler. The blood is drained away by only two large veins, the internal jugulars. So you have four arteries going up – they go up the neck of course – and two veins coming down. Around the brain itself they naturally branch out into other channels, but those don't concern us. We never touch them."

"All right," I said. "Imagine that I've just died. Now what would you do?"

"I should immediately open your neck and locate the four arteries, the carotids and the vertebrals. I should then perfuse them, which means that I'd stick a large hollow needle into each. These four needles would be connected by tubes to the artificial heart.

3f. **vascular and venous arrangement:** Anordnung der Gefäße und Venen.
7 **to be derived from s.th.:** aus etwas herstammen, kommen.
7f. **internal carotid artery:** Karotis, innere Halsschlagader.
8 **vertebral:** vertebral, zur Wirbelsäule gehörend.
12 **to drain away:** weg-, ableiten.
12f. **jugular:** Jugularvene, Halsader.
15 **to branch out:** sich verzweigen.
19 **to locate:** lokalisieren, orten.
21 **to perfuse:** durchschwemmen, künstlich durchbluten.
22 **hollow needle:** Hohlnadel.
23 **tube:** Schlauch, Röhre.

Then, working quickly, I would dissect out both the left and right jugular veins and hitch these also to the heart machine to complete the circuit. Now switch on the machine, which is already primed with the right type of blood, and there you are. The circulation through your brain would be restored."

"I'd be like that Russian dog."

"I don't think you would. For one thing, you'd certainly lose consciousness when you died, and I very much doubt whether you would come to again for quite a long time – if indeed you came to at all. But, conscious or not, you'd be in a rather interesting position, wouldn't you? You'd have a cold dead body and a living brain."

Landy paused to savour this delightful prospect. The man was so entranced and bemused by the whole idea that he evidently found it impossible to believe I might not be feeling the same way.

"We could now afford to take our time," he said. "And believe me, we'd need it. The first thing we'd do would be to wheel you to the operating-room, accompanied of course by the machine, which must never stop pumping. The next problem . . ."

"All right," I said. "That's enough. I don't have to hear the details."

1 **to dissect:** freilegen.
2 **to hitch:** eine Verbindung herstellen, befestigen.
3 **circuit:** Kreislauf.
4 **to prime:** hier: füllen, versehen.
6 **to restore:** wiederherstellen.
10 **to come to:** zu sich kommen.
14 **to savour:** genießen, auskosten.
prospect: Aussicht.
15 **entranced:** begeistert, außer sich.
bemused: gedankenverloren, vertieft; verwirrt.

"Oh but you must," he said. "It is important that you should know precisely what is going to happen to you all the way through. You see, afterwards, when you regain consciousness, it will be much more satisfactory from your point of view if you are able to remember exactly *where* you are and *how* you came to be there. If only for your own peace of mind you should know that. You agree?"

I lay still on the bed, watching him.

"So the next problem would be to remove your brain, intact and undamaged, from your dead body. The body is useless. In fact it has already started to decay. The skull and the face are also useless. They are both encumbrances and I don't want them around. All I want is the brain, the clean beautiful brain, alive and perfect. So when I get you on the table I will take a saw, a small oscillating saw, and with this I shall proceed to remove the whole vault of your skull. You'd still be unconscious at that point so I wouldn't have to bother with anaesthetic."

"Like hell you wouldn't," I said.

"You'd be out cold, I promise you that, William. Don't forget you *died* just a few minutes before."

"Nobody's sawing off the top of my skull without an anaesthetic," I said.

3 **to regain:** wiedererlangen.
7 **peace of mind:** Beruhigung, Seelenfrieden.
11 **undamaged:** unbeschädigt, unversehrt.
13 f. **encumbrance:** Hindernis.
17 **oscillating:** oszillierend, schwingend.
18 **vault:** hier: Dach.
19 f. **anaesthetic:** Betäubungsmittel.
21 **Like hell you wouldn't:** etwa: Nur über meine Leiche!
22 **to be out cold** (slang): bewußtlos sein.

Landy shrugged his shoulders. "It makes no difference to me," he said. "I'll be glad to give you a little procaine if you want it. If it will make you any happier I'll infiltrate the whole scalp with procaine, the whole head, from the neck up."

"Thanks very much," I said.

"You know," he went on, "it's extraordinary what sometimes happens. Only last week a man was brought in unconscious, and I opened his head without any anaesthetic at all and removed a small blood clot. I was still working inside the skull when he woke up and began talking.

'Where am I?' he asked.

'You're in hospital.'

'Well,' he said. 'Fancy that.'

'Tell me,' I asked him, 'is this bothering you, what I'm doing?'

'No,' he answered. 'Not at all. What *are* you doing?'

'I'm just removing a blood clot from your brain.'

'You *are*?'

'Just lie still. Don't move. I'm nearly finished.'

'So that's the bastard who's been giving me all those headaches,' the man said."

Landy paused and smiled, remembering the occasion. "That's word for word what the man said," he went on,

1 **to shrug one's shoulders:** mit den Achseln zucken.
2 **procaine:** Procain (örtliches Betäubungsmittel).
3 **to infiltrate:** (durch)tränken.
4 **scalp:** Kopfhaut, -schwarte.
10 **blood clot:** Blutgerinnsel (*clot:* Klümpchen).
15 **Fancy that!:** Stell dir vor!
16 **to bother:** plagen, quälen.
22 **bastard** (vulg.): Biest, Miststück.

"although the next day he couldn't even recollect the incident. It's a funny thing, the brain."

"I'll have the procaine," I said.

"As you wish, William. And now, as I say, I'd take a small oscillating saw and carefully remove your complete calvarium – the whole vault of the skull. This would expose the top half of the brain, or rather the outer covering in which it is wrapped. You may or may not know that there are three separate coverings around the brain itself – the outer one called the dura mater or dura, the middle one called the arachnoid, and the inner one called the pia mater or pia. Most laymen seem to have the idea that the brain is a naked thing floating around in fluid in your head. But it isn't. It's wrapped up neatly in these three strong coverings, and the cerebrospinal fluid actually flows within the little gap between the two coverings, known as the subarachnoid space. As I told you before, this fluid is manufactured by the brain and it drains off into the venous system by osmosis.

I myself would leave all three coverings – don't they have lovely names, the dura, the arachnoid, and the pia? – I'd

1 **to recollect s.th.:** sich an etwas erinnern, sich auf etwas besinnen.
6 **calvarium:** Schädeldach.
7 **to expose:** freilegen.
7 f. **covering:** Umhüllung.
10 **dura mater:** Dura mater (harte Hirn- und Rückenmarkshaut).
11 **arachnoid:** Arachnoidea (Spinngewebshaut; mittlere Hirnhaut).
12 **pia mater:** Pia mater (weiche Hirnhaut).
layman: Laie.
16 **gap:** Lücke, Hohlraum, Zwischenraum.
17 **subarachnoid space:** Subarachnoidalraum.
19 **osmosis:** Osmose (für die Stoffwechselfunktion bedeutsamer Vorgang, bei dem ein Konzentrationsaustausch zwischen verschieden starken Körperflüssigkeiten durch die Zellwände erfolgt).

leave them all intact. There are many reasons for this, not least among them being the fact that within the dura run the venous channels that drain the blood from the brain into the jugular."

"Now," he went on, "we've got the upper half of your skull off so that the top of the brain, wrapped in its outer covering, is exposed. The next step is the really tricky one: to release the whole package so that it can be lifted cleanly away, leaving the stubs of the four supply arteries and the two veins hanging underneath ready to be reconnected to the machine. This is an immensely lengthy and complicated business involving the delicate chipping away of much bone, the severing of many nerves, and the cutting and tying of numerous blood vessels. The only way I could do it with any hope of success would be by taking a rongeur and slowly biting off the rest of your skull, peeling it off downward like an orange until the sides and underneath of the brain covering are fully exposed. The problems involved are highly technical and I won't go into them, but I feel fairly sure that the work can be done. It's simply a question of surgical skill and patience. And don't forget that I'd have plenty of time, as much as I wanted, because the artificial heart would be continually pumping away alongside the operating-table, keeping the brain alive.

7 **tricky:** heikel; schwierig.
8 **to release:** befreien.
9 **stub:** Stummel, Stumpf.
11 **lengthy:** sehr lang, zeitraubend.
12 **to chip:** abschälen, -spänen.
14 **blood vessel:** Blutgefäß.
16 **rongeur:** Knochenzange, Hohlmeißelzange.
17 **to peel:** schälen.

Now, let's assume that I've succeeded in peeling off your skull and removing everything else that surrounds the sides of the brain. That leaves it connected to the body only at the base, mainly by the spinal column and by the two large veins and the four arteries that are supplying it with blood. So what next?

I would sever the spinal column just above the first cervical vertebra, taking great care not to harm the two vertebral arteries which are in that area. But you must remember that the dura or outer covering is open at this place to receive the spinal column, so I'd have to close this opening by sewing the edges of the dura together. There'd be no problem there.

At this point, I would be ready for the final move. To one side, on a table, I'd have a basin of a special shape, and this would be filled with what we call Ringer's Solution. That is a special kind of fluid we use for irrigation in neurosurgery. I would now cut the brain completely loose by severing the supply arteries and the veins. Then I would simply pick it up in my hands and transfer it to the basin. This would be the only other time during the whole proceeding when the blood flow would be cut off; but once it was in the basin, it wouldn't take a moment to re-connect the stubs of the arteries and veins to the artificial heart."

7 **spinal column:** Wirbelsäule, Rückgrat.

7 f. **cervical:** zervikal (den Hals oder Nacken betreffend).

8 **vertebra:** Wirbel.

16 **Ringer's Solution:** Ringer-Lösung (nach dem britischen Arzt und Pharmakologen S. Ringer [1835–1910] benannte, blutähnliche wäßrige Lösung, die früher als Plasmaersatz verwendet wurde).

17 **irrigation:** Irrigation, Spülung.

20 **to transfer:** hinübertragen, verlegen.

22 **proceeding:** Verfahren, Vorgehen.

"So there you are," Landy said. "Your brain is now in the basin, and still alive, and there isn't any reason why it shouldn't stay alive for a very long time, years and years perhaps, provided we looked after the blood and the machine."

"But would it *function*?"

"My dear William, how should I know? I can't even tell you whether it would regain consciousness."

"And if it did?"

"There now! That would be fascinating!"

"Would it?" I said, and I must admit I had my doubts.

"Of course it would! Lying there with all your thinking processes working beautifully, and your memory as well . . ."

"And not being able to see or feel or smell or hear or talk," I said.

"Ah!" he cried. "I knew I'd forgotten something! I never told you about the eye. Listen. I am going to try to leave one of your optic nerves intact, as well as the eye itself. The optic nerve is a little thing about the thickness of a clinical thermometer and about two inches in length as it stretches between the brain and the eye. The beauty of it is that it's not really a nerve at all. It's an outpouching of the brain itself, and the dura or brain covering extends along it and is attached to the eyeball. The back of the eye is therefore in very close contact with the brain, and cerebrospinal fluid flows right up to it.

All this suits my purpose very well, and makes it reasonable to suppose that I could succeed in preserving one of

10 **there now!:** etwa: na, dann!, tja!
19 **optic nerve:** Sehnerv.
21 **clinical:** klinisch.
23 **outpouching:** Ausstülpung.

your eyes. I've already constructed a small plastic case to contain the eyeball, instead of your own socket, and when the brain is in the basin, submerged in Ringer's Solution, the eyeball in its case will float on the surface of the liquid."

"Staring at the ceiling," I said.

"I suppose so, yes. I'm afraid there wouldn't be any muscles there to move it around. But it might be sort of fun to lie there so quietly and comfortably peering out at the world from your basin."

"Hilarious," I said. "How about leaving me an ear as well?"

"I'd rather not try an ear this time."

"I want an ear," I said. "I insist upon an ear."

"No."

"I want to listen to Bach."

"You don't understand how difficult it would be," Landy said gently. "The hearing apparatus – the cochlea, as it's called – is a far more delicate mechanism than the eye. What's more, it is encased in bone. So is a part of the auditory nerve that connects it with the brain. I couldn't possibly chisel the whole thing out intact."

"Couldn't you leave it encased in the bone and bring the bone to the basin?"

"No," he said firmly. "This thing is complicated enough

2 **socket:** (Augen-)Höhle.
3 **to submerge:** ein-, untertauchen.
9 **to peer at s.th.:** sich etwas genau ansehen.
11 **hilarious:** heiter.
14 **to insist upon s.th.:** auf etwas bestehen.
18 **cochlea:** Schnecke (des Innenohres).
20 **encased:** eingeschlossen, umschlossen.
21 **auditory nerve:** Gehörnerv.
22 **to chisel:** meißeln.

already. And anyway, if the eye works, it doesn't matter all that much about your hearing. We can always hold up messages for you to read. You really must leave me to decide what is possible and what isn't."

"I haven't yet said that I'm going to do it."

"I know, William, I know."

"I'm not sure I fancy the idea very much."

"Would you rather be dead, altogether?"

"Perhaps I would. I don't know yet. I wouldn't be able to talk, would I?"

"Of course not."

"Then how would I communicate with you? How would you know that I'm conscious?"

"It would be easy for us to know whether or not you regain consciousness," Landy said. "The ordinary electro-encephalograph could tell us that. We'd attach the electrodes directly to the frontal lobes of your brain, there in the basin."

"And you could actually tell?"

"Oh, definitely. Any hospital could do that part of it."

"But *I* couldn't communicate with *you*."

"As a matter of fact," Landy said, "I believe you could. There's a man up in London called Wertheimer who's doing some interesting work on the subject of thought communication, and I've been in touch with him. You know, don't you, that the thinking brain throws off electrical and chemical discharges? And that these dis-

15 f. **electro-encephalograph:** Elektroenzephalograph (Apparat zur Messung der Hirnaktionsströme).

17 **electrode:** Elektrode (den Stromübergang vermittelnder Leiter). **frontal lobe:** Vorderlappen.

27 **discharge:** Entladung.

charges go out in the form of waves, rather like radio waves?"

"I know a bit about it," I said.

"Well, Wertheimer has constructed an apparatus somewhat similar to the encephalograph, though far more sensitive, and he maintains that within certain narrow limits it can help him to interpret the actual things that a brain is thinking. It produces a kind of graph which is apparently decipherable into words or thoughts. Would you like me to ask Wertheimer to come and see you?"

"No," I said. Landy was already taking it for granted that I was going to go through with this business, and I resented his attitude. "Go away now and leave me alone," I told him. "You won't get anywhere by trying to rush me."

He stood up at once and crossed to the door.

"One question," I said.

He paused with a hand on the doorknob. "Yes, William?"

"Simply this. Do you yourself honestly believe that when my brain is in that basin, my mind will be able to function exactly as it is doing at present? Do you believe that I will be able to think and reason as I can now? And will the power of memory remain?"

"I don't see why not," he answered. "It's the same brain.

6 **sensitive:** empfindlich.
8 **graph:** graphische Aufzeichnung, Diagramm.
9 **apparently** (adv.): offenbar, augenscheinlich.
decipherable: entzifferbar.
11 **to take s.th. for granted:** etwas als selbstverständlich betrachten.
12 **to go through with s.th.:** etwas zu Ende führen.
13 **to resent s.th.:** etwas übelnehmen, sich an etwas stören.
15 **to rush s.o.:** jdn. treiben, drängen.

It's alive. It's undamaged. In fact, it's completely untouched. We haven't even opened the dura. The big difference, of course, would be that we've severed every single nerve that leads into it – except for the one optic nerve – and this means that your thinking would no longer be influenced by your senses. You'd be living in an extraordinarily pure and detached world. Nothing to bother you at all, not even pain. You couldn't possibly feel pain because there wouldn't be any nerves to feel it with. In a way, it would be an almost perfect situation. No worries or fears or pains or hunger or thirst. Not even any desires. Just your memories and your thoughts, and if the remaining eye happened to function, then you could read books as well. It all sounds rather pleasant to me."

"It does, does it?"

"Yes, William, it does. And particularly for a Doctor of Philosophy. It would be a tremendous experience. You'd be able to reflect upon the ways of the world with a detachment and a serenity that no man had ever attained before. And who knows what might not happen then! Great thoughts and solutions might come to you, great ideas that could revolutionize our way of life! Try to imagine, if you can, the degree of concentration that you'd be able to achieve!"

"And the frustration," I said.

7 **detached:** losgelöst; objektiv.
11 **worry:** Sorge.
18 **tremendous** (coll.): ungeheuer, außerordentlich.
20 **detachment:** Objektivität.
serenity: heitere Gelassenheit.
to attain: erlangen, erreichen.
23 **to revolutionize:** revolutionieren, von Grund auf umgestalten.
26 **frustration:** Enttäuschung, Entsagung.

"Nonsense. There couldn't be any frustration. You can't have frustration without desire, and you couldn't possibly have any desire. Not physical desire, anyway."

"I should certainly be capable of remembering my previous life in the world, and I might desire to return to it."

"What, to this mess! Out of your comfortable basin and back into this madhouse!"

"Answer one more question," I said. "How long do you believe you could keep it alive?"

"The brain? Who knows? Possibly for years and years. The conditions would be ideal. Most of the factors that cause deterioration would be absent, thanks to the artificial heart. The blood-pressure would remain constant at all times, an impossible condition in real life. The temperature would also be constant. The chemical composition of the blood would be near perfect. There would be no impurities in it, no virus, no bacteria, nothing. Of course it's foolish to guess, but I believe that a brain might live for two or three hundred years in circumstances like these. Good-bye for now," he said. "I'll drop in and see you tomorrow." He went out quickly, leaving me, as you might guess, in a fairly disturbed state of mind.

My immediate reaction after he had gone was one of revulsion towards the whole business. Somehow, it wasn't at all nice. There was something basically repulsive about the idea that I myself, with all my mental faculties intact, should be reduced to a small slimy blob

12 **deterioration:** Verschleiß.
17 **impurity:** Verunreinigung, Unreinheit.
25 **revulsion:** Ekel, Abscheu.
27 f. **mental faculty:** seelische oder geistige Fähigkeit, Geistesgabe.
28 **slimy:** schleimig.
blob: Klümpchen.

lying in a pool of water. It was monstrous, obscene, unholy. Another thing that bothered me was the feeling of helplessness that I was bound to experience once Landy had got me into the basin. There could be no going back after that, no way of protesting or explaining. I would be committed for as long as they could keep me alive.

And what, for example, if I could not stand it? What if it turned out to be terribly painful? What if I became hysterical?

No legs to run away on. No voice to scream with. Nothing. I'd just have to grin and bear it for the next two centuries.

No mouth to grin with either.

At this point, a curious thought struck me, and it was this: Does not a man who has had a leg amputated often suffer from the delusion that the leg is still there? Does he not tell the nurse that the toes he doesn't have any more are itching like mad, and so on and so forth? I seemed to have heard something to that effect quite recently.

Very well. On the same premise, was it not possible that my brain, lying there alone in that basin, might not suffer from a similar delusion in regard to my body? In which case, all my usual aches and pains could come flooding over me and I wouldn't even be able to take an aspirin to

1 **monstrous:** ungeheuerlich.
obscene: obszön.
2 **unholy** (coll.): scheußlich, schockierend.
6 **to be committed:** ausgeliefert sein.
12 **to grin and bear it:** gute Miene zum bösen Spiel machen.
16 **to amputate:** amputieren.
17 **delusion:** Einbildung, Wahn.
19 **to itch:** jucken.
21 **premise:** Voraussetzung.

relieve them. One moment I might be imagining that I had the most excruciating cramp in my leg, or a violent indigestion, and a few minutes later, I might easily get the feeling that my poor bladder – you know me – was so full that if I didn't get to emptying it soon it would burst.

Heaven forbid.

I lay there for a long time thinking these horrid thoughts. Then quite suddenly, round about midday, my mood began to change. I became less concerned with the unpleasant aspect of the affair and found myself able to examine Landy's proposals in a more reasonable light. Was there not, after all, I asked myself, something a bit comforting in the thought that my brain might not necessarily have to die and disappear in a few weeks' time? There was indeed. I am rather proud of my brain. It is a sensitive, lucid, and uberous organ. It contains a prodigious store of information, and it is still capable of producing imaginative and original theories. As brains go, it is a damn good one, though I say it myself. Whereas my body, my poor old body, the thing that Landy wants to throw away – well, even you, my dear Mary, will have to agree with me that there is really nothing about *that* which is worth preserving any more.

I was lying on my back eating a grape. Delicious it was, and there were three little seeds in it which I took out of my mouth and placed on the edge of the plate.

2 **excruciating:** qualvoll; schauderhaft.
3 **indigestion:** Verdauungsstörung.
4 **bladder:** Blase.
8 **horrid:** schrecklich, scheußlich.
17 **lucid:** hell, klar.
uberous: fruchtbar.
17f. **prodigious:** erstaunlich, wunderbar; ungewöhnlich.

"I'm going to do it," I said quietly. "Yes, by God, I'm going to do it. When Landy comes back to see me tomorrow I shall tell him straight out that I'm going to do it."

It was as quick as that. And from then on, I began to feel very much better. I surprised everyone by gobbling an enormous lunch, and shortly after that you came in to visit me as usual.

But how well I looked, you told me. How bright and well and chirpy. Had anything happened? Was there some good news?

Yes, I said there was. And then, if you remember, I bade you sit down and make yourself comfortable, and I began immediately to explain to you as gently as I could what was in the wind.

Alas, you would have none of it. I had hardly begun telling you the barest details when you flew into a fury and said that the thing was revolting, disgusting, horrible, unthinkable, and when I tried to go on, you marched out of the room.

Well, Mary, as you know, I have tried to discuss this subject with you many times since then, but you have consistently refused to give me a hearing. Hence this note, and I can only hope that you will have the good sense to permit yourself to read it. It has taken me a long time to write. Two weeks have gone since I started to scribble the first sentence, and I'm now a good deal

5 **to gobble:** hinunterschlingen.
9 **chirpy** (coll.): quietschvergnügt, lustig.
16 **to fly into a fury:** in Zorn geraten, wütend werden.
17 **revolting:** abstoßend.
disgusting: ekelhaft, widerwärtig.
22 **consistently** (adv.): durchwegs.
26 **to scribble:** kritzeln, (hin)schmieren.

weaker than I was then. I doubt whether I have the strength to say much more. Certainly I won't say good-bye, because there's a chance, just a tiny chance, that if Landy succeeds in his work I may actually *see* you again later, that is if you can bring yourself to come and visit me.

I am giving orders that these pages shall not be delivered to you until a week after I am gone. By now, therefore, as you sit reading them, seven days have already elapsed since Landy did the deed. You yourself may even know what the outcome has been. If you don't, if you have purposely kept yourself apart and have refused to have anything to do with it – which I suspect may be the case – please change your mind now and give Landy a call to see how things went with me. That is the least you can do. I have told him that he may expect to hear from you on the seventh day.

Your faithful husband,
William

PS. Be good when I am gone, and always remember that it is harder to be a widow than a wife. Do not drink cocktails. Do not waste money. Do not smoke cigarettes. Do not eat pastry. Do not use lipstick. Do not buy a television apparatus. Keep my rose beds and my rockery well weeded in the summers. And incidentally I suggest that you have the telephone disconnected now that I shall have no further use for it.

W.

9 **to elapse:** vergehen, verstreichen.
11 **outcome:** Ergebnis, Folge.
23 **pastry:** feines Gebäck, Torte(n).
25 **weeded:** frei von Unkraut.
incidentally (adv.): übrigens, nebenbei bemerkt.
26 **to disconnect:** abschalten.

Mrs Pearl laid the last page of the manuscript slowly down on the sofa beside her. Her little mouth was pursed up tight and there was a whiteness around her nostrils. But really! You would think a widow was entitled to a bit of peace after all these years.

The whole thing was just too awful to think about. Beastly and awful. It gave her the shudders.

She reached for her bag and found herself another cigarette. She lit it, inhaling the smoke deeply and blowing it out in clouds all over the room. Through the smoke she could see her lovely television set, brand new, lustrous, huge, crouching defiantly but also a little self-consciously on top of what used to be William's worktable. What would he say, she wondered, if he could see that now?

She paused, to remember the last time he had caught her smoking a cigarette. That was about a year ago, and she was sitting in the kitchen by the open window having a quick one before he came home from work. She'd had the radio on loud playing dance music and she had turned round to pour herself another cup of coffee and there he was standing in the doorway, huge and grim, staring

2 **to purse:** zusammenziehen, zusammenpressen.
3 **nostril:** Nasenloch.
4 **to be entitled to s.th.:** zu etwas berechtigt sein, ein Recht auf etwas haben.
7 **beastly** (coll.): scheußlich.
It gave her the shudders: Es überlief sie kalt. Es schauderte sie.
9 **to inhale:** inhalieren, einatmen.
11 f. **lustrous** (fig.): erstklassig, ausgezeichnet.
12 **to crouch:** hocken, kauern.
defiantly (adv.): trotzig, herausfordernd.
12 f. **self-consciously** (adv.): befangen, gehemmt, schuldbewußt.
22 **grim:** finster, düster, grimmig.

down at her with those awful eyes, a little black dot of fury blazing in the centre of each.

For four weeks after that, he had paid the housekeeping bills himself and given her no money at all, but of course he wasn't to know that she had over six pounds salted away in a soap-flake carton in the cupboard under the sink.

"What is it?" she had said to him once during supper. "Are you worried about me getting lung cancer?"

"I am not," he had answered.

"Then why can't I smoke?"

"Because I disapprove, that's why."

He had also disapproved of children, and as a result they had never had any of them either.

Where was he now, this William of hers, the great disapprover?

Landy would be expecting her to call up. Did she *have* to call Landy?

Well, not really, no.

She finished her cigarette, then lit another one immediately from the old stub. She looked at the telephone that was sitting on the worktable beside the television set. William had asked her to call. He had specifically requested that she telephone Landy as soon as she had read the letter. She hesitated, fighting hard now against that old ingrained sense of duty that she didn't quite yet

1 **dot:** Punkt, Fleck.
3 f. **housekeeping bill:** Haushaltsrechnung.
5 f. **to salt away** (slang): auf die hohe Kante legen.
6 **soap-flake carton:** Seifenflockenschachtel.
12 **to disapprove:** mißbilligen.
23 **specifically** (adv.): ausdrücklich.
26 **ingrained:** tief verwurzelt.

dare to shake off. Then, slowly, she got to her feet and crossed over to the phone on the worktable. She found a number in the book, dialled it, and waited.

"I want to speak to Mr Landy, please."

"Who is calling?"

"Mrs Pearl. Mrs William Pearl."

"One moment, please."

Almost at once, Landy was on the other end of the wire.

"Mrs Pearl?"

"This is Mrs Pearl."

There was a slight pause.

"I am so glad you called at last, Mrs Pearl. You are quite well, I hope?" The voice was quiet, unemotional, courteous. "I wonder if you would care to come over here to the hospital? Then we can have a little chat. I expect you are very eager to know how it all came out."

She didn't answer.

"I can tell you now that everything went pretty smoothly, one way and another. Far better, in fact, than I was entitled to hope. It is not only alive, Mrs Pearl, it is conscious. It recovered consciousness on the second day. Isn't that interesting?"

She waited for him to go on.

"And the eye is seeing. We are sure of that because we get an immediate change in the deflections on the encephalograph when we hold something up in front of it. And now we're giving it the newspaper to read every day."

3 **to dial:** (eine Telefonnummer) wählen.
13 **unemotional:** nüchtern, teilnahmslos, ruhig.
13 f. **courteous:** höflich, verbindlich.
25 **deflection:** hier: Kurvenbild.

"Which newspaper?" Mrs Pearl asked sharply.

"The *Daily Mirror*. The headlines are larger."

"He hates the *Mirror*. Give him *The Times*."

There was a pause, then the doctor said, "Very well, Mrs Pearl. We'll give it *The Times*. We naturally want to do all we can to keep it happy."

"*Him*," she said. "Not *it*. *Him!*"

"Him," the doctor said. "Yes, I beg your pardon. To keep him happy. That's one reason why I suggested you should come along here as soon as possible. I think it would be good for him to see you. You could indicate how delighted you were to be with him again – smile at him and blow him a kiss and all that sort of thing. It's bound to be a comfort to him to know that you are standing by."

There was a long pause.

"Well," Mrs Pearl said at last, her voice suddenly very meek and tired. "I suppose I had better come on over and see how he is."

"Good. I knew you would. I'll wait here for you. Come straight up to my office on the second floor. Good-bye."

Half an hour later, Mrs Pearl was at the hospital.

"You mustn't be surprised by what he looks like," Landy said as he walked beside her down a corridor.

"No, I won't."

"It's bound to be a bit of a shock to you at first. He's not very prepossessing in his present state, I'm afraid."

"I didn't marry him for his looks, Doctor."

Landy turned and stared at her. What a queer little

2 **Daily Mirror:** im Gegensatz zur seriösen *Times* ein Boulevardblatt.
13 **to blow s.o. a kiss:** jdm. eine Kußhand zuwerfen.
18 **meek:** mild, sanft.
27 **prepossessing:** einnehmend, gewinnend.

woman this was, he thought, with her large eyes and her sullen, resentful air. Her features, which must have been quite pleasant once, had now gone completely. The mouth was slack, the cheeks loose and flabby, and the whole face gave the impression of having slowly but surely sagged to pieces through years and years of joyless married life. They walked on for a while in silence.

"Take your time when you get inside," Landy said. "He won't know you're in there until you place your face directly above his eye. The eye is always open, but he can't move it at all, so the field of vision is very narrow. At present we have it looking up at the ceiling. And of course he can't hear anything. We can talk together as much as we like. It's in here."

Landy opened a door and ushered her into a small square room.

"I wouldn't go too close yet," he said, putting a hand on her arm. "Stay back here a moment with me until you get used to it all."

There was a biggish white enamel bowl about the size of a washbasin standing on a high white table in the centre of the room, and there were half a dozen thin plastic tubes coming out of it. These tubes were connected with a

2 **sullen:** mürrisch, verdrossen, grämlich.
resentful: verstimmt, grollend.
air: Miene, Ausdruck.
features: Gesichtszüge.
4 **slack:** schlaff.
flabby: schlaff.
6 **to sag:** sinken, fallen.
11 **field of vision:** Blick-, Gesichtsfeld.
15 **to usher:** hineinführen.
20 **biggish:** ziemlich groß.
enamel: Emaille.

whole lot of glass piping in which you could see the blood flowing to and from the heart machine. The machine itself made a soft rhythmic pulsing sound.

"He's in there," Landy said, pointing to the basin, which was too high for her to see into. "Come just a little closer. Not too near."

He led her two paces forward.

By stretching her neck, Mrs Pearl could now see the surface of the liquid inside the basin. It was clear and still, and on it there floated a small oval capsule, about the size of a pigeon's egg.

"That's the eye in there," Landy said. "Can you see it?"

"Yes."

"So far as we can tell, it is still in perfect condition. It's his right eye, and the plastic container has a lens on it similar to the one he used in his own spectacles. At this moment he's probably seeing quite as well as he did before."

"The ceiling isn't much to look at," Mrs Pearl said.

"Don't worry about that. We're in the process of working out a whole programme to keep him amused, but we don't want to go too quickly at first."

"Give him a good book."

"We will, we will. Are you feeling all right, Mrs Pearl?"

"Yes."

"Then we'll go forward a little more, shall we, and you'll be able to see the whole thing."

He led her forward until they were standing only a couple of yards from the table, and now she could see right down into the basin.

1 **piping:** Rohrleitung.
10 **capsule:** Kapsel.
11 **pigeon:** Taube.

"There you are," Landy said. "That's William."

He was far larger than she had imagined he would be, and darker in colour. With all the ridges and creases running over his surface, he reminded her of nothing so much as an enormous pickled walnut. She could see the stubs of the four big arteries and the two veins coming out from the base of him and the neat way in which they were joined to the plastic tubes; and with each throb of the heart machine, all the tubes gave a little jerk in unison as the blood was pushed through them.

"You'll have to lean over," Landy said, "and put your pretty face right above the eye. He'll see you then, and you can smile at him and blow him a kiss. If I were you I'd say a few nice things as well. He won't actually hear them, but I'm sure he'll get the general idea."

"He hates people blowing kisses at him," Mrs Pearl said. "I'll do it my own way if you don't mind." She stepped up to the edge of the table, leaned forward until her face was directly over the basin, and looked straight down into William's eye.

"Hallo, dear," she whispered. "It's me – Mary."

The eye, bright as ever, stared back at her with a peculiar, fixed intensity.

"How are you, dear?" she said.

The plastic capsule was transparent all the way round so that the whole of the eyeball was visible. The optic nerve

3 **ridge:** Furche, Wulst.
crease: Falte.
5 **pickled:** eingemacht, eingelegt.
walnut: Walnuß.
8 **throb:** Pulsieren, Pochen, Klopfen.
9 **in unison:** unisono, im Takt.
25 **transparent:** durchsichtig.

connecting the underside of it to the brain looked like a short length of grey spaghetti.

"Are you feeling all right, William?"

It was a queer sensation peering into her husband's eye when there was no face to go with it. All she had to look at was the eye, and she kept staring at it, and gradually it grew bigger and bigger, and in the end it was the only thing that she could see – a sort of face in itself. There was a network of tiny red veins running over the white surface of the eyeball, and in the ice-blue of the iris there were three or four rather pretty darkish streaks radiating from the pupil in the centre. The pupil was large and black, with a little spark of light reflecting from one side of it.

"I got your letter, dear, and came over at once to see how you were. Dr Landy says you are doing wonderfully well. Perhaps if I talk slowly you can understand a little of what I am saying by reading my lips."

There was no doubt that the eye was watching her.

"They are doing everything possible to take care of you, dear. This marvellous machine thing here is pumping away all the time and I'm sure it's a lot better than those silly old hearts all the rest of us have. Ours are liable to break down at any moment, but yours will go on for ever."

She was studying the eye closely, trying to discover what there was about it that gave it such an unusual appearance.

"You seem fine, dear, simply fine. Really you do."

It looked ever so much nicer, this eye, than either of his

11 **streak:** Streifen.
to radiate: ausstrahlen, strahlenförmig ausgehen.
22 **to be liable to:** (mit etwas) rechnen müssen.

eyes used to look, she told herself. There was a softness about it somewhere, a calm, kindly quality that she had never seen before. Maybe it had to do with the dot in the very centre, the pupil. William's pupils used always to be tiny black pinheads. They used to glint at you, stabbing into your brain, seeing right through you, and they always knew at once what you were up to and even what you were thinking. But this one she was looking at now was large and soft and gentle, almost cowlike.

"Are you quite sure he's conscious?" she asked, not looking up.

"Oh yes, completely," Landy said.

"And he *can* see me?"

"Perfectly."

"Isn't that marvellous? I expect he's wondering what happened."

"Not at all. He knows perfectly well where he is and why he's there. He can't possibly have forgotten that."

"You mean he *knows* he's in this basin?"

"Of course. And if only he had the power of speech, he would probably be able to carry on a perfectly normal conversation with you this very minute. So far as I can see, there should be absolutely no difference mentally between this William here and the one you used to know back home."

"Good *gracious* me," Mrs Pearl said, and she paused to consider this intriguing aspect.

2 **kindly:** gütig, freundlich.
5 **pinhead:** (Steck-)Nadelkopf.
to glint: funkeln.
to stab: stechen.
26 **Good gracious me:** Du meine Güte! Lieber Himmel!
27 **intriguing:** faszinierend, aufregend.

You know what, she told herself, looking behind the eye now and staring hard at the great grey pulpy walnut that lay so placidly under the water, I'm not at all sure that I don't prefer him as he is at present. In fact, I believe that I could live very comfortably with this kind of a William. I could cope with this one.

"Quiet, isn't he?" she said.

"Naturally he's quiet."

No arguments and criticisms, she thought, no constant admonitions, no rules to obey, no ban on smoking cigarettes, no pair of cold disapproving eyes watching me over the top of a book in the evenings, no shirts to wash and iron, no meals to cook – nothing but the throb of the heart machine, which was rather a soothing sound anyway and certainly not loud enough to interfere with television.

"Doctor," she said. "I do believe I'm suddenly getting to feel the most enormous affection for him. Does that sound queer?"

"I think it's quite understandable."

"He looks so helpless and silent lying there under the water in his little basin."

"Yes, I know."

"He's like a baby, that's what he's like. He's exactly like a little baby."

Landy stood still behind her, watching.

2 **pulpy:** weich, schwammig.
3 **placidly** (adv.): ruhig, friedlich, sanft.
6 **to cope with s.th.:** mit etwas fertig werden; es mit etwas aufnehmen.
9 **criticism:** Kritik.
10 **admonition:** Ermahnung.
ban: Verbot.
14 **soothing:** beruhigend.

"There," she said softly, peering into the basin. "From now on Mary's going to look after you *all* by herself and you've nothing to worry about in the world. When can I have him back home, Doctor?"

"I beg your pardon?"

"I said when can I have him back – back in my own house?"

"You're joking," Landy said.

She turned her head slowly around and looked directly at him. "Why should I joke?" she asked. Her face was bright, her eyes round and bright as two diamonds.

"He couldn't possibly be moved."

"I don't see why not."

"This is an experiment, Mrs Pearl."

"It's my husband, Dr Landy."

A funny little nervous half-smile appeared on Landy's mouth. "Well . . ." he said.

"It *is* my husband, you know." There was no anger in her voice. She spoke quietly, as though merely reminding him of a simple fact.

"That's rather a tricky point," Landy said, wetting his lips. "You're a widow now, Mrs Pearl. I think you must resign yourself to that fact."

She turned away suddenly from the table and crossed over to the window. "I mean it," she said, fishing in her bag for a cigarette. "I want him back."

Landy watched her as she put the cigarette between her lips and lit it. Unless he were very much mistaken, there was something a bit odd about this woman, he thought. She seemed almost pleased to have her husband over there in the basin.

23 **to resign o.s. to s.th.:** sich mit etwas abfinden.

He tried to imagine what his own feelings would be if it were *his* wife's brain lying there and *her* eye staring up at him out of that capsule.

He wouldn't like it.

"Shall we go back to my room now?" he said.

She was standing by the window, apparently quite calm and relaxed, puffing her cigarette.

"Yes, all right."

On her way past the table she stopped and leaned over the basin once more. "Mary's leaving now, sweetheart," she said. "And don't you worry about a single thing, you understand? We're going to get you right back home where we can look after you properly just as soon as we possibly can. And listen dear ..." At this point she paused and carried the cigarette to her lips, intending to take a puff.

Instantly the eye flashed.

She was looking straight into it at the time, and right in the centre of it she saw a tiny but brilliant flash of light, and the pupil contracted into a minute black pinpoint of absolute fury.

At first she didn't move. She stood bending over the basin, holding the cigarette up to her mouth, watching the eye.

Then very slowly, deliberately, she put the cigarette between her lips and took a long suck. She inhaled deeply, and she held the smoke inside her lungs for three or four seconds; then suddenly, *whoosh*, out it came through her

17 **instantly** (adv.): augenblicklich, sofort.
20 **to contract:** sich zusammenziehen.
minute: winzig.
25 **deliberately** (adv.): bedächtig.
26 **to take a long suck:** einen langen Zug machen.

nostrils in two thin jets which struck the water in the basin and billowed out over the surface in a thick blue cloud, enveloping the eye.

Landy was over by the door, with his back to her, waiting. “Come on, Mrs Pearl,” he called.

“Don’t look so cross, William,” she said softly. “It isn’t any good looking cross.”

Landy turned his head to see what she was doing.

“Not any more it isn’t,” she whispered. “Because from now on, my pet, you’re going to do just exactly what Mary tells you. Do you understand that?”

“Mrs Pearl,” Landy said, moving towards her.

“So don’t be a naughty boy again, will you, my precious,” she said, taking another pull at the cigarette. “Naughty boys are liable to get punished most severely nowadays, you ought to know that.”

Landy was beside her now, and he took her by the arm and began drawing her firmly but gently away from the table.

“Good-bye, darling,” she called. “I’ll be back soon.”

“That’s enough, Mrs Pearl.”

“Isn’t he sweet?” she cried, looking up at Landy with big bright eyes. “Isn’t he heaven? I just can’t wait to get him home.”

1 **jet:** Strahl.
2 **to billow:** wogen, sich türmen, ballen.
3 **to envelop:** einhüllen.
6 **cross** (coll.): ärgerlich, verdrießlich.
10 **pet:** Liebling.
13 **naughty:** ungezogen, unartig.
precious: Schatz, Liebling.
14 **to take a pull:** einen Zug machen.

The Wish

Under the palm of one hand the child became aware of the scab of an old cut on his kneecap. He bent forward to examine it closely. A scab was always a fascinating thing; it presented a special challenge he was never able to resist.

Yes, he thought, I will pick it off, even if it isn't ready, even if the middle of it sticks, even if it hurts like anything.

With a fingernail he began to explore cautiously around the edges of the scab. He got the nail underneath it, and when he raised it, but ever so slightly, it suddenly came off, the whole hard brown scab came off beautifully, leaving an interesting little circle of smooth red skin.

Nice. Very nice indeed. He rubbed the circle and it didn't hurt. He picked up the scab, put it on his thigh and flipped it with a finger so that it flew away and landed on the edge of the carpet, the enormous red and black and yellow carpet that stretched the whole length of the hall from the stairs on which he sat to the front door in the distance. A tremendous carpet. Bigger than the tennis

2 **palm:** Handfläche, -teller.
3 **scab:** Schorf, Kruste.
kneecap: Kniescheibe.
12 f. **to come off:** abgehen, sich ablösen.
16 **thigh:** (Ober-)Schenkel.
16 f. **to flip:** (weg)schnippen.
21 **tremendous:** ungeheuerlich.

lawn. Much bigger than that. He regarded it gravely, settling his eyes upon it with mild pleasure. He had never really noticed it before, but now, all of a sudden, the colours seemed to brighten mysteriously and spring out at him in a most dazzling way.

You see, he told himself, I know how it is. The red parts of the carpet are red-hot lumps of coal. What I must do is this: I must walk all the way along it to the front door without touching them. If I touch the red I will be burnt. As a matter of fact, I will be burnt up completely. And the black parts of the carpet . . . yes, the black parts are snakes, poisonous snakes, adders mostly, and cobras, thick like tree-trunks round the middle, and if I touch one of *them*, I'll be bitten and I'll die before tea time. And if I get across safely, without being burnt and without being bitten, I will be given a puppy for my birthday tomorrow.

He got to his feet and climbed higher up the stairs to obtain a better view of this vast tapestry of colour and death. Was it possible? Was there enough yellow? Yellow was the only colour he was allowed to walk on. Could it be done? This was not a journey to be undertaken lightly; the risks were too great for that. The child's face – a fringe of white-gold hair, two large blue eyes, a small pointed chin – peered down anxiously over the banisters.

5 **dazzling:** blendend, leuchtend; verwirrend.
7 **red-hot:** rotglühend.
lump: Stück, Brocken, Klumpen.
12 **poisonous:** giftig.
adder: Natter, Viper; besonders: Kreuzotter.
16 **puppy:** junger Hund.
19 **tapestry:** Tapisserie, Gewebe.
25 **to peer:** suchend schauen, in Augenschein nehmen.
banisters (pl.): Treppengeländer.

The yellow was a bit thin in places and there were one or two widish gaps, but it did seem to go all the way along to the other end. For someone who had only yesterday triumphantly travelled the whole length of the brick path from the stables to the summer-house without touching the cracks, this carpet thing should not be too difficult. Except for the snakes. The mere thought of snakes sent a fine electricity of fear running like pins down the backs of his legs and under the soles of his feet.

He came slowly down the stairs and advanced to the edge of the carpet. He extended one small sandalled foot and placed it cautiously upon a patch of yellow. Then he brought the other foot up, and there was just enough room for him to stand with the two feet together. There! He had started! His bright oval face was curiously intent, a shade whiter perhaps than before, and he was holding his arms out sideways to assist his balance. He took another step, lifting his foot high over a patch of black, aiming carefully with his toe for a narrow channel of yellow on the other side. When he had completed the second step he paused to rest, standing very stiff and still. The narrow channel of yellow ran forward unbroken for at least five yards and he advanced gingerly along it, bit by bit, as though walking a tightrope. Where it finally

2 **widish:** ziemlich breit.
gap: Spalte, Lücke.
6 **crack:** Fuge, Spalt, Ritze.
9 **sole:** Sohle.
11 **to extend:** ausstrecken.
sandalled: in Sandalen steckend.
15 **intent:** aufmerksam, gespannt, ernsthaft.
17 **sideways:** seitlich, nach der Seite.
23 **gingerly** (adv.): (übertrieben) vorsichtig, zimperlich.
24 **tightrope:** Drahtseil (von Artisten).

curled off sideways, he had to take another long stride, this time over a vicious-looking mixture of black and red. Half-way across he began to wobble. He waved his arms around wildly, windmill fashion, to keep his balance, and he got across safely and rested again on the other side. He was quite breathless now, and so tense he stood high on his toes all the time, arms out sideways, fists clenched. He was on a big safe island of yellow. There was lots of room on it, he couldn't possibly fall off, and he stood there resting, hesitating, waiting, wishing he could stay for ever on this big safe yellow island. But the fear of not getting the puppy compelled him to go on.
Step by step, he edged further ahead, and between each one he paused to decide exactly where next he should put his foot. Once, he had a choice of ways, either to left or right, and he chose the left because although it seemed the more difficult, there was not so much black in that direction. The black was what made him nervous. He glanced quickly over his shoulder to see how far he had come. Nearly half-way. There could be no turning back now. He was in the middle and he couldn't turn back and he couldn't jump off sideways either because it was too far, and when he looked at all the red and all the black that lay ahead of him, he felt that old sudden sickening

1 **to curl off:** abbiegen, abschwenken.
stride: Schritt.
2 **vicious-looking:** bösartig, tückisch aussehend.
3 **to wobble:** wackeln, schwanken, taumeln.
4 **windmill fashion:** wie eine Windmühle.
6 **tense:** (an)gespannt, verkrampft.
7 **to clench:** zusammenpressen, zur Faust ballen.
12 **to compel:** zwingen, nötigen.
13 **to edge:** (sich) langsam schieben.
24 **sickening:** Übelkeit erregend, widerwärtig.

surge of panic in his chest – like last Easter time, that afternoon when he got lost all alone in the darkest part of Piper's Wood.

He took another step, placing his foot carefully upon the only little piece of yellow within reach, and this time the point of the foot came within a centimetre of some black. It wasn't touching the black, he could see it wasn't touching, he could see the small line of yellow separating the toe of his sandal from the black; but the snake stirred as though sensing the nearness, and raised its head and gazed at the foot with bright beady eyes, watching to see if it was going to touch.

"I'm not touching you! You mustn't bite me! You know I'm not touching you!"

Another snake slid up noiselessly beside the first, raised its head, two heads now, two pairs of eyes staring at the foot, gazing at a little naked place just below the sandal strap where the skin showed through. The child went high up on his toes and stayed there, frozen stiff with terror. It was minutes before he dared to move again.

The next step would have to be a really long one. There was this deep curling river of black that ran clear across the width of the carpet, and he was forced by this position to cross it at its widest part. He thought first of trying to jump it, but decided he couldn't be sure of landing accurately on the narrow band of yellow the other side. He took a deep breath, lifted one foot, and inch by inch he

1 **surge:** Welle, Woge.
11 **beady:** perlartig.
18 **strap:** Riemen, Band.
to show through: sich zeigen, durchscheinen.
22 **clear:** hier: ungehindert.
25 f. **accurately** (adv.): genau, exakt, sorgfältig.

pushed it out in front of him, far far out, then down and down until at last the tip of his sandal was across and resting safely on the edge of the yellow. He leaned forward, transferring his weight to his front foot. Then he tried to bring the back foot up as well. He strained and pulled and jerked his body, but the legs were too wide apart and he couldn't make it. He tried to get back again. He couldn't do that either. He was doing the splits and he was properly stuck. He glanced down and saw this deep curling river of black underneath him. Parts of it were stirring now, and uncoiling and sliding and beginning to shine with a dreadfully oily glister. He wobbled, waved his arms frantically to keep his balance, but that seemed to make it worse. He was starting to go over. He was going over to the right, quite slowly he was going over, then faster and faster, and at the last moment, instinctively he put out a hand to break the fall and the next thing he saw was this bare hand of his going right into the middle of a great glistening mass of black and he gave one piercing cry of terror as it touched.

Outside in the sunshine, far away behind the house, the mother was looking for her son.

4 **to transfer:** übertragen, verlegen.
6 **to jerk:** rucken, ruckweise bewegen.
8 **to do the splits:** Spagat machen.
11 **to uncoil:** auseinanderrollen.
12 **glister:** Funkeln, Glitzern.
13 **frantically** (adv.): außer sich, wild.
19 **to glisten:** glitzern, glänzen.
20 **piercing:** schneidend, durchdringend.

Pig

1

Once upon a time, in the City of New York, a beautiful baby boy was born into this world, and the joyful parents named him Lexington.
No sooner had the mother returned home from the hospital carrying Lexington in her arms than she said to her husband, "Darling, now you must take me out to a most marvellous restaurant for dinner so that we can celebrate the arrival of our son and heir."
Her husband embraced her tenderly and told her that any woman who could produce such a beautiful child as Lexington deserved to go absolutely anywhere she wanted. But was she strong enough yet, he inquired, to start running around the city late at night?
"No," she said, she wasn't. But what the hell.
So that evening they both dressed themselves up in fancy clothes, and leaving little Lexington in care of a trained infant's nurse who was costing them twenty dollars a day and was Scottish into the bargain, they went out to the finest and most expensive restaurant in town. There they

3 **once upon a time:** es war einmal; vorzeiten.
10 **heir:** Erbe.
11 **to embrace:** umarmen.
16 **what the hell:** etwa: was soll's!
17 f. **fancy clothes** (pl.): Gala.
19 **infant's nurse:** Kindermädchen.
20 **into the bargain:** zu allem Überfluß, obendrein.

each ate a giant lobster and drank a bottle of champagne between them, and after that, they went on to a night-club, where they drank another bottle of champagne and then sat holding hands for several hours while they recalled and discussed and admired each individual physical feature of their lovely newborn son.

They arrived back at their house on the East Side of Manhattan at around two o'clock in the morning and the husband paid off the taxi driver and then began feeling in his pockets for the key to the front door. After a while, he announced that he must have left it in the pocket of his other suit, and he suggested they ring the bell and get the nurse to come down and let them in. An infant's nurse at twenty dollars a day must expect to be hauled out of bed occasionally in the night, the husband said.

So he rang the bell. They waited. Nothing happened. He rang it again, long and loud. They waited another minute. Then they both stepped back on to the street and shouted the nurse's name (McPottle) up at the nursery windows on the third floor, but there was still no response. The house was dark and silent. The wife began to grow apprehensive. Her baby was imprisoned in this place, she told herself. Alone with McPottle. And who was McPottle? They had known her for two days, that

1 **lobster:** Hummer.
champagne: Champagner.
4f. **to recall:** sich erinnern, ins Gedächtnis zurückrufen.
5 **physical:** körperlich.
6 **feature:** Merkmal.
11 **to announce:** verkünden.
14 **to haul out:** herausbefördern, -holen.
19 **nursery:** Kinderzimmer.
22 **apprehensive:** besorgt, furchtsam.
imprisoned: gefangen.

was all, and she had a thin mouth, a small disapproving eye, and a starchy bosom, and quite clearly she was in the habit of sleeping too soundly for safety. If she couldn't hear the front-door bell, then how on earth did she expect to hear a baby crying? Why, this very second the poor thing might be swallowing its tongue or suffocating on its pillow.

"He doesn't use a pillow," the husband said. "You are not to worry. But I'll get you in if that's what you want." He was feeling rather superb after all the champagne, and now he bent down and undid the laces of one of his black patent-leather shoes, and took it off. Then, holding it by the toe, he flung it hard and straight through the dining-room window on the ground floor.

"There you are," he said, grinning. "We'll deduct it from McPottle's wages."

He stepped forward and very carefully put a hand through the hole in the glass and released the catch. Then he raised the window.

"I shall lift you in first, little mother," he said, and he

1 **disapproving:** mißbilligend, tadelnd.
2 **starchy:** gestärkt (Wäsche).
bosom: Busen, Brust.
3 **soundly** (adv.): fest, tief, gesund.
5 **why:** nun, doch, ja.
6 **to swallow:** verschlucken.
6f. **to suffocate:** ersticken.
10 **superb:** großartig.
11 **to undo:** öffnen, aufbinden.
12 **patent-leather shoes:** Lackschuhe.
13 **to fling:** werfen, schleudern.
15 **There you are!:** etwa: Na also!
to deduct: abziehen.
18 **to release:** öffnen, entriegeln.
catch: Haken, Riegel.

took his wife around the waist and lifted her off the ground. This brought her big red mouth up level with his own, and very close, so he started kissing her. He knew from experience that women like very much to be kissed in this position, with their bodies held tight and their legs dangling in the air, so he went on doing it for quite a long time, and she wiggled her feet, and made loud gulping noises down in her throat. Finally, the husband turned her round and began easing her gently through the open window into the dining-room. At this point, a police patrol car came nosing silently along the street towards them. It stopped about thirty yards away, and three cops of Irish extraction leaped out of the car and started running in the direction of the husband and wife, brandishing revolvers.

"Stick 'em up!" the cops shouted. "Stick 'em up!" But it was impossible for the husband to obey this order without letting go of his wife, and had he done this she would either have fallen to the ground or would have been left dangling half in and half out of the house, which is a terribly uncomfortable position for a woman; so he con-

2 **level with:** auf gleicher Höhe mit.
6 **to dangle:** schlenkern, baumeln.
7 **to wiggle:** strampeln, sich winden.
gulping: glucksend.
9 **to ease:** langsam herunterlassen, behutsam schieben.
10 f. **patrol car:** Streifenwagen.
11 **to nose:** hier: vorsichtig, im Schrittempo fahren; sich langsam nähern.
12 **cop** (slang): Polizist, ‚Bulle'.
13 **extraction:** Herkunft, Abstammung.
14 f. **to brandish:** schwenken, schwingen; zücken.
16 **Stick 'em up!:** Hände hoch!
18 **to let go:** loslassen.
21 **uncomfortable:** unbequem, unangenehm

tinued gallantly to push her upward and inward through the window. The cops, all of whom had received medals before for killing robbers, opened fire immediately, and although they were still running, and although the wife in particular was presenting them with a very small target indeed, they succeeded in scoring several direct hits on each body – sufficient anyway to prove fatal in both cases.

Thus, when he was no more than twelve days old, little Lexington became an orphan.

2

The news of this killing, for which the three policemen subsequently received citations, was eagerly conveyed to all relatives of the deceased couple by newspaper reporters, and the next morning the closest of these relatives, as well as a couple of undertakers, three lawyers, and a priest, climbed into taxis and set out for the house with

1 **gallantly** (adv.): tapfer; ritterlich.
2 **medal:** Orden, Medaille.
3 **to open fire:** das Feuer eröffnen.
4 f. **in particular:** insbesondere.
5 **target:** Ziel.
6 **to score a hit:** treffen.
7 **sufficient:** genug, ausreichend.
fatal: tödlich.
10 **orphan:** Waise.
13 **subsequently** (adv.): nachträglich, später.
citation: Belobigung, anerkennende Erwähnung.
to convey: überbringen, übermitteln, mitteilen.
14 **relative:** Verwandte(r).
deceased: verstorben.
16 **undertaker:** Leichenbestatter.
lawyer: Anwalt.
17 **to set out for s.th.:** zu etwas aufbrechen, sich nach etwas aufmachen.

the broken window. They assembled in the living-room, men and women both, and they sat around in a circle on the sofas and armchairs, smoking cigarettes and sipping sherry and debating what on earth should be done now with the baby upstairs, the orphan Lexington.

It soon became apparent that none of the relatives was particularly keen to assume responsibility for the child, and the discussions and arguments continued all through the day. Everybody declared an enormous, almost an irresistible desire to look after him, and would have done so with the greatest of pleasure were it not for the fact that their apartment was too small, or that they already had one baby and couldn't possibly afford another, or that they went abroad in the summer, or that they were getting on in years, which surely would be most unfair to the boy when he grew up, and so on and so forth. They all knew, of course, that the father had been heavily in debt for a long time and that the house was mortgaged and that consequently there would be no money at all to go with the child.

They were still arguing like mad at six in the evening when suddenly, in the middle of it all, an old aunt of the deceased father (her name was Glosspan) swept in from

3 **armchair:** Sessel.
to sip: nippen.
4 **to debate:** diskutieren, erörtern.
6 **apparent:** offensichtlich, erkennbar.
7 **to assume:** annehmen, übernehmen.
10 **irresistible:** unwiderstehlich.
18 **mortgaged:** mit einer Hypothek belastet.
23 **Glosspan:** sprechender Name (*gloss:* Glanz; *pan:* Pfanne); Anspielung auf Pangloss, den Lehrer des Titelhelden in Voltaires 1759 erschienenem Roman *Candide ou l'Optimisme*.
to sweep in: hereinrauschen.

Virginia, and without even removing her hat and coat, not even pausing to sit down, ignoring all offers of a martini, a whisky, a sherry, she announced firmly to the assembled relatives that she herself intended to take sole charge of the infant boy from then on. What was more, she said, she would assume full financial responsibility on all counts, including education, and everyone else could go back home where they belonged and give their consciences a rest. So saying, she trotted upstairs to the nursery and snatched Lexington from his cradle and swept out of the house with the baby clutched tightly in her arms, while the relatives simply sat and stared and smiled and looked relieved, and McPottle the nurse stood stiff with disapproval at the head of the stairs, her lips compressed, her arms folded across her starchy bosom.

And thus it was that the infant Lexington, when he was thirteen days old, left the City of New York and travelled southward to live with his Great Aunt Glosspan in the State of Virginia.

3

Aunt Glosspan was nearly seventy when she became guardian to Lexington, but to look at her you would never have guessed it for one minute. She was as

1 **to remove:** (Kleidungsstück) ablegen.
4f. **to take charge of s.o.:** Verantwortung für jdn. übernehmen.
sole: alleinig.
9 **to trot:** traben, eilen.
10 **cradle:** Wiege.
11 **to clutch:** fassen, umklammern.
14 **disapproval:** Mißbilligung.
compressed: zusammengepreßt, zusammengekniffen.
22 **guardian:** Vormund.

sprightly as a woman half her age, with a small, wrinkled, but still quite beautiful face and two lovely brown eyes that sparkled at you in the nicest way. She was also a spinster, though you would never have guessed that either, for there was nothing spinsterish about Aunt Glosspan. She was never bitter or gloomy or irritable; she didn't have a moustache; and she wasn't in the least bit jealous of other people, which in itself is something you can seldom say about either a spinster or a virgin lady, although of course it is not known for certain whether Aunt Glosspan qualified on both counts.

But she was an eccentric old woman, there was no doubt about that. For the past thirty years she had lived a strange isolated life all by herself in a tiny cottage high up on the slopes of the Blue Ridge Mountains, several miles from the nearest village. She had five acres of pasture, a plot for growing vegetables, a flower garden, three cows, a dozen hens, and a fine cockerel.

And now she had little Lexington as well.

1 **sprightly:** lebhaft, munter.
wrinkled: runzlig, von Falten durchzogen.
3 **to sparkle:** funkeln, glitzern, blitzen.
4 **spinster:** unverheiratete Frau, (alte) Jungfer.
5 **spinsterish:** altjüngferlich.
6 **gloomy:** düster, trübselig; mürrisch.
irritable: reizbar, empfindlich.
7 **moustache:** Schnurrbart.
9 **virgin:** Jungfrau; jungfräulich.
11 **whether . . . qualified on both counts:** ob beides auf . . . zutraf.
12 **eccentric:** exzentrisch, wunderlich.
15 **slope:** (Ab-)Hang
16 **acre:** angelsächsische Flächeneinheit (etwa 4047 qm).
pasture: Weideland.
17 **plot:** Stückchen, Flecken.
18 **cockerel:** junger Hahn.

She was a strict vegetarian and regarded the consumption of animal flesh as not only unhealthy and disgusting, but horribly cruel. She lived upon lovely clean foods like milk, butter, eggs, cheese, vegetables, nuts, herbs, and fruit, and she rejoiced in the conviction that no living creature would be slaughtered on her account, not even a shrimp. Once, when a brown hen of hers passed away in the prime of life from being eggbound, Aunt Glosspan was so distressed that she nearly gave up egg-eating altogether.

She knew not the first thing about babies, but that didn't worry her in the least. At the railway station in New York, while waiting for the train that would take her and Lexington back to Virginia, she bought six feeding-bottles, two dozen diapers, a box of safety pins, a carton of milk for the journey, and a small paper-covered book called *The Care of Infants*. What more could anyone want? And when the train got going, she fed the baby

1 **vegetarian:** Vegetarier(in).
1f. **consumption:** Genuß, Verzehr.
2 **disgusting:** ekelhaft, widerwärtig.
4 **herb:** (Heil-)Kraut.
5 **to rejoice:** sich (er)freuen, glücklich sein.
conviction: Überzeugung, Bewußtsein.
6 **to slaughter:** schlachten.
7 **shrimp:** Garnele, Krabbe.
to pass away: verscheiden, versterben.
8 **prime of life:** Blüte des Lebens.
to be eggbound: Legenot haben.
9 **distressed:** bekümmert, unglücklich.
11 **not to know the first thing about s.th.:** von etwas nichts verstehen.
14f. **feeding-bottle:** Babyfläschchen.
15 **diaper:** Windel.
16 **paper-covered:** broschiert.

some milk, changed its nappies after a fashion, and laid it down on the seat to sleep. Then she read *The Care of Infants* from cover to cover.

"There is no problem here," she said, throwing the book out of the window. "No problem at all."

And curiously enough there wasn't. Back home in the cottage everything went just as smoothly as could be. Little Lexington drank his milk and belched and yelled and slept exactly as a good baby should, and Aunt Glosspan glowed with joy whenever she looked at him and showered him with kisses all day long.

4

By the time he was six years old, young Lexington had grown into a most beautiful boy with long golden hair and deep blue eyes the colour of cornflowers. He was bright and cheerful, and already he was learning to help his old aunt in all sorts of different ways around the property, collecting the eggs from the chicken house, turning the handle of the butter churn, digging up potatoes in the vegetable garden, and searching for wild herbs on the side of the mountain. Soon, Aunt Glosspan told herself, she would have to start thinking about his education. But she couldn't bear the thought of sending him away to

1 **nappy** (coll.): Windel.
after a fashion: hier: so gut sie konnte; nach bestem Wissen.
8 **to belch:** aufstoßen, rülpsen.
to yell: brüllen, schreien.
11 **to shower:** überschütten, überhäufen.
15 **cornflower:** Kornblume.
17 f. **property:** Besitz, Grundstück.
19 **butter churn:** Butterfaß.

school. She loved him so much now that it would kill her to be parted from him for any length of time. There was, of course, that village school down in the valley, but it was a dreadful-looking place, and if she sent him there she just knew they would start forcing him to eat meat the very first day he arrived.

"You know what, my darling?" she said to him one day when he was sitting on a stool in the kitchen watching her make cheese. "I don't really see why I shouldn't give you your lessons myself."

The boy looked up at her with his large blue eyes, and gave her a lovely trusting smile. "That would be nice," he said.

"And the very first thing I should do would be to teach you how to cook."

"I think I would like that, Aunt Glosspan."

"Whether you like it or not, you're going to have to learn some time," she said. "Vegetarians like us don't have nearly so many foods to choose from as ordinary people, and therefore they must learn to be doubly expert with what they have."

"Aunt Glosspan," the boy said, "what *do* ordinary people eat that we don't?"

"Animals," she answered, tossing her head in disgust.

"You mean *live* animals?"

"No," she said. "Dead ones."

The boy considered this for a moment.

2 **for any length of time:** längere Zeit.
8 **stool:** Hocker, Schemel.
12 **trusting:** vertrauensvoll.
20 **expert:** erfahren, kundig.
24 **to toss:** schütteln.
25 **live:** lebend.

"You mean when they die they *eat* them instead of *burying* them?"

"They don't wait for them to die, my pet. They kill them."

"How do they kill them, Aunt Glosspan?"

"They usually slit their throats with a knife."

"But what *kind* of animals?"

"Cows and pigs mostly, and sheep."

"Cows!" the boy cried. "You mean like Daisy and Snowdrop and Lily?"

"Exactly, my dear."

"But *how* do they eat them, Aunt Glosspan?"

"They cut them up into bits and they cook the bits. They like it best when it's all red and bloody and sticking to the bones. They love to eat lumps of cow's flesh with the blood oozing out of it."

"Pigs too?"

"They adore pigs."

"Lumps of bloody pig's meat," the boy said. "Imagine that. What else do they eat, Aunt Glosspan?"

"Chickens."

"Chickens!"

"Millions of them."

"Feathers and all?"

"No, dear, not the feathers. Now run along outside and

3 **pet:** Liebling.
6 **to slit:** aufschlitzen, aufschneiden.
9 **daisy:** Gänseblümchen.
9f. **snowdrop:** Schneeglöckchen.
10 **lily:** Lilie.
15 **lump:** Klumpen, Brocken.
16 **to ooze out:** heraussickern, -rinnen.
18 **to adore s.th.** (coll.): für etwas schwärmen.

get Aunt Glosspan a bunch of chives, will you, my darling."

Shortly after that, the lessons began. They covered five subjects, reading, writing, geography, arithmetic, and cooking, but the latter was by far the most popular with both teacher and pupil. In fact, it very soon became apparent that young Lexington possessed a truly remarkable talent in this direction. He was a born cook. He was dextrous and quick. He could handle his pans like a juggler. He could slice a single potato into twenty paper-thin slivers in less time than it took his aunt to peel it. His palate was exquisitely sensitive, and he could taste a pot of strong onion soup and immediately detect the presence of a single tiny leaf of sage. In so young a boy, all this was a bit bewildering to Aunt Glosspan, and to tell the truth she didn't quite know what to make of it. But she was proud as proud could be, all the same, and predicted a brilliant future for the child.

"What a mercy it is," she said, "that I have such a wonderful little fellow to look after me in my dotage." And a

1 **chives** (pl.): Schnittlauch.
4 **arithmetic:** Rechnen.
5 **latter:** letzteres.
9 **dextrous:** gewandt, geschickt.
9 f. **juggler:** Jongleur, Zauberkünstler.
10 **to slice:** in Scheiben schneiden.
11 **sliver:** Scheibchen.
to peel: schälen.
12 **palate:** Gaumen.
exquisitely (adv.): außerordentlich, überaus.
sensitive: empfindlich.
14 **sage:** Salbei.
17 f. **to predict:** vorhersagen, prophezeien.
19 **mercy:** Gnade, Segen.
20 **in my dotage:** auf meine alten Tage.

couple of years later, she retired from the kitchen for good, leaving Lexington in sole charge of all household cooking. The boy was now ten years old, and Aunt Glosspan was nearly eighty.

5

With the kitchen to himself, Lexington straight away began experimenting with dishes of his own invention. The old favourites no longer interested him. He had a violent urge to create. There were hundreds of fresh ideas in his head. "I will begin," he said, "by devising a chestnut soufflé." He made it and served it up for supper that very night. It was terrific. "You are a genius!" Aunt Glosspan cried, leaping up from her chair and kissing him on both cheeks. "You will make history!" From then on, hardly a day went by without some new delectable creation being set upon the table. There was Brazilnut soup, hominy cutlets, vegetable ragout, dandelion omelette, cream-cheese fritters, stuffed-cabbage

1 **to retire:** sich zurückziehen.
1 f. **for good:** für immer, endgültig.
9 **urge:** Drang.
10 **to devise:** erfinden, sich ausdenken.
11 **chestnut soufflé:** Kastaniensoufflé.
12 **terrific** (coll.): kolossal, großartig, fabelhaft.
16 **delectable:** köstlich, lecker.
17 **Brazilnut:** Paranuß.
hominy cutlets: Koteletts aus grob gemahlenem Mais.
17 f. **dandelion:** Löwenzahn.
18 **fritter:** Fettgebackenes mit Füllung.
18 f. **stuffed-cabbage surprise:** gefüllter Kohl mit Überraschung (*surprise* [frz.]: Überraschung).

surprise, stewed foggage, shallots *à la bonne femme*, beetroot mousse piquant, prunes Stroganoff, Dutch rarebit, turnips on horseback, flaming spruce-needle tarts, and many many other beautiful compositions. Never before in her life, Aunt Glosspan declared, had she tasted such food as this; and in the mornings, long before lunch was due, she would go out on to the porch and sit there in her rocking-chair, speculating about the coming meal, licking her chops, sniffing the aromas that came wafting out through the kitchen window.

"What's that you're making in there today, boy?" she would call out.

"Try to guess, Aunt Glosspan."

"Smells like a bit of salsify fritters to me," she would say, sniffing vigorously.

1 **to stew:** schmoren, dämpfen, dünsten.
foggage: Spätheu, Grummet.
shallot: Schalotte (kleine Ziebel).
à la bonne femme (frz.): nach Art der Hausfrau.
2 **beetroot:** rote Bete.
mousse (frz.): Schaum, Creme.
piquant (frz.): pikant.
prune: Pflaume.
2f. **Dutch rarebit:** abgeleitet von *Welsh rarebit* ›mit Käse überbackene Weißbrotscheibe‹.
3 **turnips on horseback:** panierte Rübenschnitzel.
flaming: flammend (*flaming* [slang] ›verdammt‹ schwingt wohl mit).
3f. **spruce-needle tart:** Fichtennadelpastete.
7 **to be due:** zu erwarten, fällig sein.
porch: Veranda (AE).
8 **rocking-chair:** Schaukelstuhl.
to speculate: Vermutungen anstellen.
9 **to lick one's chops:** sich die Lippen lecken.
10 **to waft:** wehen.
14 **salsify:** lauchblättriger Bocksbart.
15 **vigorously** (adv.): kräftig.

Then out he would come, this ten-year-old child, a little grin of triumph on his face, and in his hands a big steaming pot of the most heavenly stew made entirely of parsnips and lovage.

"You know what you ought to do," his aunt said to him, gobbling the stew. "You ought to set yourself down this very minute with paper and pencil and write a cooking-book."

He looked at her across the table, chewing his parsnips slowly.

"Why not?" she cried. "I've taught you how to write and I've taught you how to cook and now all you've got to do is put the two things together. You write a cooking-book, my darling, and it'll make you famous the whole world over."

"All right," he said. "I will."

And that very day, Lexington began writing the first page of that monumental work which was to occupy him for the rest of his life. He called it *Eat Good and Healthy*.

6

Seven years later, by the time he was seventeen, he had recorded over nine thousand different recipes, all of them original, all of them delicious.

But now, suddenly, his labours were interrupted by the

2 **grin:** Grinsen.
3 **stew:** Schmorgericht, Eintopf.
3f. **parsnip:** Pastinak.
4 **lovage:** Liebstöckel.
6 **to gobble:** ver-, hinunterschlingen.
9 **to chew:** kauen.
22 **recipe:** Kochrezept.
23 **delicious:** köstlich, wohlschmeckend.

tragic death of Aunt Glosspan. She was afflicted in the night by a violent seizure, and Lexington, who had rushed into her bedroom to see what all the noise was about, found her lying on her bed yelling and cussing and twisting herself up into all manner of complicated knots. Indeed, she was a terrible sight to behold, and the agitated youth danced around her in his pyjamas, wringing his hands, and wondering what on earth he should do. Finally, in an effort to cool her down, he fetched a bucket of water from the pond in the cow field and tipped it over her head, but this only intensified the paroxysms, and the old lady expired within the hour.

"This is really too bad," the poor boy said, pinching her several times to make sure that she was dead. "And how sudden! How quick and sudden! Why only a few hours ago she seemed in the very best of spirits. She even took three large helpings of my most recent creation, devilled mushroomburgers, and told me how succulent it was."

After weeping bitterly for several minutes, for he had loved his aunt very much, he pulled himself together

1f. **to be afflicted by s.th.:** von etwas erfaßt werden, an etwas leiden.
2 **seizure:** plötzlicher Anfall.
4 **to cuss:** verfluchen, verwünschen.
5 **to twist:** sich winden.
6f. **agitated:** aufgewühlt, verstört, sehr aufgeregt.
10 **to tip over:** aus-, umkippen.
11 **to intensify:** verstärken.
paroxysm: Krampf, Anfall.
12 **to expire:** verscheiden, sterben.
13 **to pinch:** zwicken, kneifen.
17 **helping:** Portion.
devilled: fein zerhackt und scharf gewürzt; teuflisch.
18 **mushroomburgers:** Pilzbouletten.
succulent: saftig.

and carried her outside and buried her behind the cowshed.

The next day, while tidying up her belongings, he came across an envelope that was addressed to him in Aunt Glosspan's handwriting. He opened it and drew out two fifty-dollar bills and a letter.

Darling boy [the letter said], I know that you have never yet been down the mountain since you were thirteen days old, but as soon as I die you must put on a pair of shoes and a clean shirt and walk down to the village and find the doctor. Ask the doctor to give you a death certificate to prove that I am dead. Then take this certificate to my lawyer, a man called Mr Samuel Zuckermann, who lives in New York City and who has a copy of my will. Mr Zuckermann will arrange everything. The cash in this envelope is to pay the doctor for the certificate and to cover the cost of your journey to New York. Mr Zuckermann will give you more money when you get there, and it is my earnest wish that you use it to further your researches into culinary and vegetarian matters, and that you continue to work upon that great book of yours until you are satisfied that it is complete in every way. Your loving aunt – Glosspan.

Lexington, who had always done everything his aunt told him, pocketed the money, put on a pair of shoes and a clean shirt, and went down the mountain to the village where the doctor lived.

2 **cowshed:** Kuhstall.
3 **to tidy up:** aufräumen, in Ordnung bringen.
belongings: Habseligkeiten, Sachen.
11 **death certificate:** Totenschein.
14 **will:** Testament.
18 **to further:** fördern, unterstützen.
research: Forschung.
23 **to pocket:** einstecken.

"Old Glosspan?" the doctor said. "My God, is *she* dead?"

"Certainly she's dead," the youth answered. "If you will come back home with me now I'll dig her up and you can see for yourself."

"How deep did you bury her?" the doctor asked.

"Six or seven feet down, I should think."

"And how long ago?"

"Oh, about eight hours."

"Then she's dead," the doctor announced. "Here's the certificate."

7

Our hero now sets out for the City of New York to find Mr Samuel Zuckermann. He travelled on foot, and he slept under hedges, and he lived on berries and wild herbs, and it took him sixteen days to reach the metropolis.

"What a fabulous place this is!" he cried as he stood at the corner of Fifty-seventh Street and Fifth Avenue, staring around him. "There are no cows or chickens anywhere, and none of the women looks in the least like Aunt Glosspan."

As for Mr Samuel Zuckermann, he looked like nothing that Lexington had ever seen before.

He was a small spongy man with livid jowls and a huge

16f. **metropolis:** Metropole, Hauptstadt.
18 **fabulous** (coll.): fabelhaft.
25 **spongy:** aufgedunsen, schwammig.
livid: fahl, bleich.
jowl: Wange.

magenta nose, and when he smiled, bits of gold flashed at you marvellously from lots of different places inside his mouth. In his luxurious office, he shook Lexington warmly by the hand and congratulated him upon his aunt's death.

"I suppose you knew that your dearly beloved guardian was a woman of considerable wealth?" he said.

"You mean the cows and the chickens?"

"I mean half a million bucks," Mr Zuckermann said.

"How much?"

"Half a million dollars, my boy. And she's left it all to you." Mr Zuckermann leaned back in his chair and clasped his hands over his spongy paunch. At the same time, he began secretly working his right forefinger in through his waistcoat and under his shirt so as to scratch the skin around the circumference of his navel – a favourite exercise of his, and one that gave him a peculiar pleasure. "Of course, I shall have to deduct fifty per cent for my services," he said, "but that still leaves you with two hundred and fifty grand."

"I am rich!" Lexington cried. "This is wonderful! How soon can I have the money?"

"Well," Mr Zuckermann said, "luckily for you, I happen to be on rather cordial terms with the tax authorities

1 **magenta:** magentarot.
4 **warmly** (adv.): freundlich, herzlich.
6 **beloved:** geliebt.
9 **buck** (slang): Dollar.
13 **paunch:** Wanst.
15 **waistcoat:** Weste.
16 **circumference:** Umkreis.
navel: Nabel.
20 **grand** (slang): tausend Dollar.
24 **cordial:** herzlich, freundschaftlich.

around here, and I am confident that I shall be able to persuade them to waive all death duties and back taxes."

"How kind you are," murmured Lexington.

"I should naturally have to give somebody a small honorarium."

"Whatever you say, Mr Zuckermann."

"I think a hundred thousand would be sufficient."

"Good gracious, isn't that rather excessive?"

"Never undertip a tax inspector or a policeman," Mr Zuckermann said. "Remember that."

"But how much does it leave for me?" the youth asked meekly.

"One hundred and fifty thousand. But then you've got the funeral expenses to pay out of that."

"*Funeral* expenses?"

"You've got to pay the funeral parlour. Surely you know that?"

"But I buried her myself, Mr Zuckermann, behind the cowshed."

"I don't doubt it," the lawyer said. "So what?"

"I never used a funeral parlour."

"Listen," Mr Zuckermann said patiently. "You may not know it, but there is a law in this State which says that no beneficiary under a will may receive a single penny of his

2 **to waive s.th.:** auf etwas verzichten.
death duty: Erbschafts-, Nachlaßsteuer.
back tax: Steuerschuld.
4f. **honorarium:** Honorar.
8 **good gracious:** du meine Güte!
9 **to undertip:** zu wenig Trinkgeld geben.
12 **meekly** (adv.): bescheiden, sanft.
14 **funeral expenses:** Bestattungskosten.
16 **funeral parlour:** Bestattungsinstitut.
24 **beneficiary:** Empfänger einer Erbschaft.

inheritance until the funeral parlour has been paid in full."

"You mean that's a *law*?"

"Certainly it's a law, and a very good one it is, too. The funeral parlour is one of our great national institutions. It must be protected at all costs."

Mr Zuckermann himself, together with a group of public-spirited doctors, controlled a corporation that owned a chain of nine lavish funeral parlours in the city, not to mention a casket factory in Brooklyn and a postgraduate school for embalmers in Washington Heights. The celebration of death was therefore a deeply religious affair in Mr Zuckermann's eyes. In fact, the whole business affected him profoundly, almost as profoundly, one might say, as the birth of Christ affected the shopkeeper.

"You had no right to go out and bury your aunt like that," he said. "None at all."

"I'm very sorry, Mr Zuckermann."

"Why, it's downright subversive."

"I'll do whatever you say, Mr Zuckermann. All I want to know is how much I'm going to get in the end, when everything's paid."

There was a pause. Mr Zuckermann sighed and frowned

1 **inheritance:** Erbschaft.
7 f. **public-spirited:** auf das Gemeinwohl bedacht.
8 **corporation:** Gesellschaft, Unternehmen.
9 **lavish:** luxuriös, verschwenderisch.
10 **casket:** Sarg (AE).
10 f. **postgraduate school:** etwa: Fortbildungsinstitut.
11 **embalmer:** Einbalsamierer.
15 f. **shopkeeper:** Krämer, Ladenbesitzer.
20 **downright:** völlig, durch und durch.
subversive: subversiv, umstürzlerisch.

and continued secretly to run the tip of his finger around the rim of his navel.

"Shall we say fifteen thousand?" he suggested, flashing a big gold smile. "That's a nice round figure."

"Can I take it with me this afternoon?"

"I don't see why not."

So Mr Zuckermann summoned his chief cashier und told him to give Lexington fifteen thousand dollars out of the petty cash, and to obtain a receipt. The youth, who by this time was delighted to be getting anything at all, accepted the money gratefully and stowed it away in his knapsack. Then he shook Mr Zuckermann warmly by the hand, thanked him for all his help, and went out of the office.

"The whole world is before me!" our hero cried as he emerged into the street. "I now have fifteen thousand dollars to see me through until my book is published. And after that, of course, I shall have a great deal more."

He stood on the pavement, wondering which way to go. He turned left and began strolling slowly down the street, staring at the sights of the city.

"What a revolting smell," he said, sniffing the air. "I

2 **rim:** Rand.
7 **to summon:** rufen, kommen lassen.
chief cashier: Hauptkassier.
9 **petty cash:** Handkasse.
receipt: Quittung.
11 **to stow away:** verstauen.
12 **knapsack:** Rucksack, Ranzen.
16 **to emerge:** herauskommen, hinaustreten.
17 **to see s.o. through:** jdm. durchhelfen.
20 **to stroll:** bummeln, schlendern.
22 **revolting:** abstoßend.

can't stand this." His delicate olfactory nerves, tuned to receive only the most delicious kitchen aromas, were being tortured by the stench of the diesel-oil fumes pouring out of the backs of the buses.

"I must get out of this place before my nose is ruined altogether," he said. "But first, I've simply got to have something to eat. I'm starving." The poor boy had had nothing but berries and wild herbs for the past two weeks, and now his stomach was yearning for solid food. I'd like a nice hominy cutlet, he told himself. Or maybe a few juicy salsify fritters.

He crossed the street and entered a small restaurant. The place was hot inside, and dark and silent. There was a strong smell of cooking-fat and cabbage water. The only other customer was a man with a brown hat on his head, crouching intently over his food, who did not look up as Lexington came in.

Our hero seated himself at a corner table and hung his knapsack on the back of his chair. This, he told himself, is going to be most interesting. In all my seventeen years I have tasted only the cooking of two people, Aunt Glosspan and myself – unless one counts Nurse McPottle, who must have heated my bottle a few times when I was an infant. But I am now about to sample the art of a new chef altogether, and perhaps, if I am lucky, I may pick up a couple of useful ideas for my book.

1 **olfactory nerves:** Geruchsnerven.
to tune: abstimmen, einstellen.
3 **stench:** Gestank.
fumes (pl.): Schwaden.
9 **to yearn for s.th.:** sich nach etwas sehnen.
16 **to crouch:** hocken; sich beugen.
intently (adv.): ernstlich beschäftigt, hingegeben.
24 **to sample:** probieren, kosten.

A waiter approached out of the shadows at the back, and stood beside the table.

"How do you do," Lexington said. "I should like a large hominy cutlet please. Do it twenty-five seconds each side, in a very hot skillet with sour cream, and sprinkle a pinch of lovage on it before serving – unless of course your chef knows of a more original method, in which case I should be delighted to try it."

The waiter laid his head over to one side and looked carefully at his customer. "You want the roast pork and cabbage?" he asked. "That's all we got left."

"Roast what and cabbage?"

The waiter took a soiled handkerchief from his trouser pocket and shook it open with a violent flourish, as though he were cracking a whip. Then he blew his nose loud and wet.

"You want it or don't you?" he said, wiping his nostrils.

"I haven't the foggiest idea what it is," Lexington replied, "but I should love to try it. You see, I am writing a cooking-book and . . ."

"One pork and cabbage!" the waiter shouted, and somewhere in the back of the restaurant, far away in the darkness, a voice answered him.

The waiter disappeared. Lexington reached into his knapsack for his personal knife and fork. These were a present from Aunt Glosspan, given him when he was six

5 **skillet:** Pfanne.
to sprinkle: streuen.
6 **pinch:** Prise.
10 **roast pork:** Schweinebraten.
13 **soiled:** schmutzig, verschmutzt.
14 **flourish:** Schwung.
15 **to crack:** knallen lassen.

years old, made of solid silver, and he had never eaten with any other instruments since. While waiting for the food to arrive, he polished them lovingly with a piece of soft muslin.

Soon the waiter returned carrying a plate on which there lay a thick greyish-white slab of something hot. Lexington leaned forward anxiously to smell it as it was put down before him. His nostrils were wide open now to receive the scent, quivering and sniffing.

"But this is absolute heaven!« he exclaimed. "What an aroma! It's tremendous!"

The waiter stepped back a pace, watching his customer carefully.

"Never in my life have I smelled anything as rich and wonderful as this!" our hero cried, seizing his knife and fork. "What on earth is it made of?"

The man in the brown hat looked around and stared, then returned to his eating. The waiter was backing away towards the kitchen.

Lexington cut off a small piece of the meat, impaled it on his silver fork, and carried it up to his nose so as to smell it again. Then he popped it into his mouth and began to chew it slowly, his eyes half closed, his body tense.

"This is fantastic!" he cried. "It is a brand-new flavour!

3 **lovingly** (adv.): liebevoll.
4 **muslin:** Musselin (Baumwollstoff).
6 **slab:** Scheibe.
9 **scent:** Geruch.
to quiver: zittern, beben.
11 **tremendous:** ungeheuerlich.
20 **to impale:** aufspießen.
22 **to pop:** schnell stecken.
23 **tense:** gespannt.
24 **flavour:** Geschmack, Aroma.

Oh, Glosspan, my beloved Aunt, how I wish you were with me now so you could taste this remarkable dish! Waiter! Come here at once! I want you!"

The astonished waiter was now watching from the other end of the room, and he seemed reluctant to move any closer.

"If you will come and talk to me I will give you a present," Lexington said, waving a hundred-dollar bill. "Please come over here and talk to me."

The waiter sidled cautiously back to the table, snatched away the money, and held it up close to his face, peering at it from all angles. Then he slipped it quickly into his pocket.

"What can I do for you, my friend?" he asked.

"Look," Lexington said. "If you will tell me what this delicious dish is made of, and exactly how it is prepared, I will give you another hundred."

"I already told you," the man said. "It's pork."

"And what exactly is pork?"

"You never had roast pork before?" the waiter asked, staring.

"For heaven's sake, man, tell me what it is and stop keeping me in suspense like this."

"It's pig," the waiter said. "You just bung it in the oven."

"Pig!"

"All pork is pig. Didn't you know that?"

"You mean *this* is *pig's* meat?"

5 **reluctant:** zögernd, widerstrebend.
10 **to sidle:** schleichen, sich schlängeln.
11 f. **to peer at s.th.:** sich etwas genau ansehen.
23 **suspense:** Ungewißheit, Spannung.
24 **to bung** (slang): schmeißen.
oven: (Brat-, Back-)Ofen.

"I guarantee it."

"But . . . but . . . that's impossible," the youth stammered. "Aunt Glosspan, who knew more about food than anyone else in the world, said that meat of any kind was disgusting, revolting, horrible, foul, nauseating, and beastly. And yet this piece that I have here on my plate is without doubt the most delicious thing that I have ever tasted. Now how on earth do you explain that? Aunt Glosspan certainly wouldn't have told me it was revolting if it wasn't."

"Maybe your aunt didn't know how to cook it," the waiter said.

"Is that possible?"

"You're damned right it is. Especially with pork. Pork has to be very well done or you can't eat it."

"Eureka!" Lexington cried. "I'll bet that's exactly what happened! She did it wrong!" He handed the man another hundred-dollar bill. "Lead me to the kitchen," he said. "Introduce me to the genius who prepared this meat."

Lexington was at once taken into the kitchen, and there he met the cook who was an elderly man with a rash on one side of his neck.

"This will cost you another hundred," the waiter said.

Lexington was only too glad to oblige, but this time he gave the money to the cook. "Now listen to me," he said. "I have to admit that I am really rather confused by what the waiter has just been telling me. Are you quite posi-

5 **nauseating:** ekelerregend.
6 **beastly** (coll.): abscheulich.
22 **rash:** (Haut-)Ausschlag.
25 **to oblige:** zu Gefallen sein.
28 f. **positive:** sicher.

tive that the delectable dish which I have just been eating was prepared from pig's flesh?"

The cook raised his right hand and began scratching the rash on his neck.

"Well," he said, looking at the waiter and giving him a sly wink, "all I can tell you is that I *think* it was pig's meat."

"You mean you're not sure?"

"One can't ever be sure."

"Then what else could it have been?"

"Well," the cook said, speaking very slowly and still staring at the waiter. "There's just a chance, you see, that it might have been a piece of human stuff."

"You mean a man?"

"Yes."

"Good heavens."

"Or a woman. It could have been either. They both taste the same."

"Well – now you really do surprise me," the youth declared.

"One lives and learns."

"Indeed one does."

"As a matter of fact, we've been getting an awful lot of it just lately from the butcher's in place of pork," the cook declared.

"Have you really?"

"The trouble is, it's almost impossible to tell which is which. They're both very good."

"The piece I had just now was simply superb."

"I'm glad you liked it," the cook said. "But to be quite honest, I think that was a bit of pig. In fact, I'm almost sure it was."

5 **sly:** verstohlen, heimlich.

"You are?"

"Yes, I am."

"In that case, we shall have to assume that you are right," Lexington said. "So now will you please tell me – and here is another hundred dollars for your trouble – will you please tell me precisely how you prepared it?"

The cook, after pocketing the money, launched out upon a colourful description of how to roast a loin of pork, while the youth, not wanting to miss a single word of so great a recipe, sat down at the kitchen table and recorded every detail in his notebook.

"Is that all?" he asked when the cook had finished.

"That's all."

"But there must be more to it than that, surely?"

"You got to get a good piece of meat to start off with," the cook said. "That's half the battle. It's got to be a good hog and it's got to be butchered right, otherwise it'll turn out lousy whichever way you cook it."

"Show me how," Lexington said. "Butcher me one now so I can learn."

"We don't butcher pigs in the kitchen," the cook said. "That lot you just ate came from a packing-house over in the Bronx."

"Then give me the address!"

The cook gave him the address, and our hero, after thanking them both many times for all their kindnesses, rushed outside and leapt into a taxi and headed for the Bronx.

7 **to launch out:** (einen Wortschwall) von sich geben.
8 **loin:** Lende.
17 **hog:** Schwein.
18 **lousy** (slang): widerlich, abscheulich.
22 **packing-house** (AE): Konservenfabrik.
27 **to head for s.th.:** auf etwas zusteuern.

8

The packing-house was a big four-storey brick building, and the air around it smelled sweet and heavy, like musk. At the main entrance gates, there was a large notice which said VISITORS WELCOME AT ANY TIME, and thus encouraged, Lexington walked through the gates and entered a cobbled yard which surrounded the building itself. He then followed a series of signposts (THIS WAY FOR THE GUIDED TOURS), and came eventually to a small corrugated-iron shed set well apart from the main building (VISITORS' WAITING-ROOM). After knocking politely on the door, he went in.

There were six other people ahead of him in the waiting-room. There was a fat mother with her two little boys aged about nine and eleven. There was a bright-eyed young couple who looked as though they might be on their honeymoon. And there was a pale woman with long white gloves, who sat very upright, looking straight ahead, with her hands folded on her lap. Nobody spoke. Lexington wondered whether they were all writing cooking-books, like himself, but when he put this question to them aloud, he got no answer. The grown-ups merely smiled mysteriously to themselves and shook their heads, and the two children stared at him as though they were seeing a lunatic.

Soon, the door opened and a man with a merry pink face popped his head into the room and said, "Next, please." The mother and the two boys got up and went out.

3 **musk:** Moschus.
7 **cobbled:** gepflastert.
8 **signpost:** Wegweiser.
10 **corrugated-iron shed:** Wellblechschuppen.
25 **lunatic:** Geisteskranker, Verrückter.

About ten minutes later, the same man returned. "Next, please," he said again, and the honeymoon couple jumped up and followed him outside.

Two new visitors came in and sat down – a middle-aged husband and a middle-aged wife, the wife carrying a wicker shopping-basket containing groceries.

"Next, please," said the guide, and the woman with the long white gloves got up and left.

Several more people came in and took their places on the stiff-backed wooden chairs.

Soon the guide returned for the third time, and now it was Lexington's turn to go outside.

"Follow me, please," the guide said, leading the youth across the yard towards the main building.

"How exciting this is!" Lexington cried, hopping from one foot to the other. "I only wish that my dear Aunt Glosspan could be with me now to see what I am going to see."

"I myself only do the preliminaries," the guide said. "Then I shall hand you over to someone else."

"Anything you say," cried the ecstatic youth.

First they visited a large penned-in area at the back of the building where several hundred pigs were wandering around. "Here's where they start," the guide said. "And over there's where they go in."

"Where?"

"Right there." The guide pointed to a long wooden shed

6 **wicker:** geflochten, Weiden-.
groceries (pl.): Lebensmittel.
15 **to hop:** hüpfen.
19 **preliminaries** (pl.): Einleitung.
21 **ecstatic:** begeistert.
22 **penned-in:** eingezäunt.

that stood against the outside wall of the factory. "We call it the shackling-pen. This way, please."

Three men wearing long rubber boots were driving a dozen pigs into the shackling-pen just as Lexington and the guide approached, so they all went in together.

"Now," the guide said, "watch how they shackle them."

Inside, the shed was simply a bare wooden room with no roof, and there was a steel cable with hooks on it that kept moving slowly along the length of one wall, parallel with the ground, about three feet up. When it reached the end of the shed, this cable suddenly changed direction and climbed vertically upward through the open roof towards the top floor of the main building.

The twelve pigs were huddled together at the far end of the pen, standing quietly, looking apprehensive. One of the men in rubber boots pulled a length of metal chain down from the wall and advanced upon the nearest animal, approaching it from the rear. Then he bent down and quickly looped one end of the chain around one of the animal's hind legs. The other end he attached to a hook on the moving cable as it went by. The cable kept moving. The chain tightened. The pig's leg was pulled up and back, and then the pig itself began to be dragged backwards. But it didn't fall down. It was rather a nimble pig, and somehow it managed to keep its balance on three legs, hopping from foot to foot and struggling against the pull of the chain, but going back and back all

2 **shackling-pen:** Pferch, in dem die Tiere an das Transportkabel gekettet werden (*to shackle:* anketten, fesseln; *pen:* Gehege).

14 **to huddle:** zusammendrängen.

19 **to loop:** schlingen.

23 **to drag:** zerren, schleifen.

24 **nimble:** flink, behend.

the time until at the end of the pen where the cable changed direction and went vertically upward, the creature was suddenly jerked off its feet and borne aloft. Shrill protests filled the air.

"Truly a fascinating process," Lexington said. "But what was the funny cracking noise it made as it went up?"

"Probably the leg," the guide answered. "Either that or the pelvis."

"But doesn't that matter?"

"Why should it matter?" the guide asked. "You don't eat the bones."

The rubber-booted men were busy shackling the rest of the pigs, and one after another they were hooked to the moving cable and hoisted up through the roof, protesting loudly as they went.

"There's a good deal more to this recipe than just picking herbs," Lexington said. "Aunt Glosspan would never have made it."

At this point, while Lexington was gazing skyward at the last pig to go up, a man in rubber boots approached him quietly from behind and looped one end of a chain around the youth's own ankle, hooking the other end to the moving belt. The next moment, before he had time to realize what was happening, our hero was jerked off his feet and dragged backwards along the concrete floor of the shackling-pen.

"Stop!" he cried. "Hold everything! My leg is caught!"

3 **to jerk:** reißen, ruckartig ziehen.
aloft (poet.): in die Höhe, empor.
8 **pelvis:** Becken.
14 **to hoist up:** hoch-, hinaufziehen.
23 **belt:** *conveyor-belt:* Transportband.
25 **concrete:** Beton.

But nobody seemed to hear him, and five seconds later, the unhappy young man was jerked off the floor and hoisted vertically upward through the open roof of the pen, dangling upside down by one ankle, and wriggling like a fish.

"Help!" he shouted. "Help! There's been a frightful mistake! Stop the engines! Let me down!"

The guide removed a cigar from his mouth and looked up serenely at the rapidly ascending youth, but he said nothing. The men in rubber boots were already on their way out to collect the next batch of pigs.

"Oh, save me!" our hero cried. "Let me down! Please let me down!" But he was now approaching the top floor of the building where the moving belt curled over like a snake and entered a large hole in the wall, a kind of doorway without a door; and there, on the threshold, waiting to greet him, clothed in a dark-stained yellow rubber apron, and looking for all the world like Saint Peter at the Gates of Heaven, the sticker stood.

Lexington saw him only from upside down, and very briefly at that, but even so he noticed at once the expression of absolute peace and benevolence on the man's face, the cheerful twinkle in the eyes, the little wistful smile, the dimples in his cheeks – and all this gave him hope.

4 **to wriggle:** sich winden, zappeln.
9 **serenely** (adv.): ruhig, gelassen.
11 **batch:** Menge, Trupp; Schub; Stoß.
14 **to curl over:** etwa: eine scharfe Biegung machen.
17 **dark-stained:** mit dunklen Flecken.
19 **sticker:** Stecher, Schlächter.
22 **benevolence:** Güte, Wohlwollen.
23 **wistful:** nachdenklich, versonnen.
24 **dimple:** Grübchen.

"Hi there," the sticker said, smiling.

"Quick! Save me!" our hero cried.

"With pleasure," the sticker said, and taking Lexington gently by one ear with his left hand, he raised his right hand and deftly slit open the boy's jugular vein with a knife.

The belt moved on. Lexington went with it. Everything was still upside down and the blood was pouring out of his throat and getting into his eyes, but he could still see after a fashion, and he had a blurred impression of being in an enormously long room, and at the far end of the room there was a great smoking cauldron of water, and there were dark figures, half hidden in the steam, dancing around the edge of it, brandishing long poles. The conveyor-belt seemed to be travelling right over the top of the cauldron, and the pigs seemed to be dropping down one by one into the boiling water, and one of the pigs seemed to be wearing long white gloves on its front feet.

Suddenly our hero started to feel very sleepy, but it wasn't until his good strong heart had pumped the last drop of blood from his body that he passed on out of this, the best of all possible worlds, into the next.

5 **deftly** (adv.): flink, geschickt.
jugular vein: Halsschlagader.
10 **blurred:** verschwommen.
12 **cauldron:** großer Kessel.
14 **pole:** Stange.
23 **the best of all possible worlds:** weitere Anspielung auf *Candide*.

Zeittafel zu Leben und Werk von Roald Dahl

1916 Am 13. September in Llandaff (Südwales) geboren.
1920 Tod des Vaters, Harald Dahl, eines norwegischen Kaufmanns.
1925 Besuch der St. Peter's School, Weston-super-Mare (Somerset).
1929 Weitere Erziehung in der Repton Public School (Schauplatz der autobiographischen Erzählung »Galloping Foxley«).
1933 Dahl, der kein Interesse an einem Universitätsstudium hat, bewirbt sich erfolgreich bei der Shell Oil Company.
1936 Nach einer Ausbildung in England erhält er die ersehnte Versetzung nach Afrika (Daressalam).
1939 Bei Kriegsausbruch freiwillige Meldung zur Royal Air Force.
1939–41 Einsatz in Libyen, Griechenland und Syrien. Nach schwerer Verwundung als »Assistant Air Attaché« nach Washington.
1942 Begegnung mit C. S. Forester, die zur Veröffentlichung seiner ersten Geschichte, »A Piece of Cake«, führt.
1943 Nach Erscheinen des Kinderbuchs *The Gremlins* vorübergehend Zusammenarbeit mit Walt Disney. Bis Kriegsende Tätigkeit für den britischen Geheimdienst.
1945 Dahl schreibt für *The New Yorker, Collier's, Harper's Magazine* und die *Saturday Evening Post.*
1946 *Over to You*, Dahls erste Kurzgeschichtensammlung.
1948 Der Roman *Some Time Never. A Fable for Supermen* wird von der Kritik kühl aufgenommen.
1953 Heirat mit der Schauspielerin Patricia Neal. Die erfolgreiche Kurzgeschichtensammlung *Someone Like You* erscheint.
1959 Veröffentlichung der Kurzgeschichtensammlung *Kiss Kiss*, die ein besonders positives Echo in der Kritik findet.
1961 Dahl beginnt, regelmäßig Kinderbücher zu schreiben.
1967–71 Arbeit als Drehbuchautor.
1974 *Switch Bitch*, vier Erzählungen »this or the other side of pornography« (Umschlagtext).
1979 *My Uncle Oswald* (Roman), eine Art Fortsetzung der Erzählung »Bitch« aus *Switch Bitch*.
1984 *Boy, Tales of Childhood*, eine bebilderte Autobiographie.
1985 Deutscher Jugendbuchpreis für die Übersetzung des Kinderbuchs *The BFG* (1982, dt. *Sophiechen und der Riese*).
1986 *Going Solo* setzt die mit *Boy* begonnenen Memoiren fort.

Roald Dahl lebt mit seinen vier Kindern in Gipsy House, Great Missenden (Buckinghamshire).

Nachwort

Roald Dahl ist ein Bestsellerautor.[1] Allein die Kurzgeschichtensammlungen *Kiss Kiss* und *Someone Like You* haben in deutscher Übersetzung eine Auflage von zwei Millionen erreicht. Die Rezeptur dieses Erfolges scheint leicht zu ergründen: »If your taste is for the macabre, the sick, the outrageous, the unexpected, the horrifying – Roald Dahl will give you orgiastic delight« (Verlagswerbung). Wer zöge nicht gerne aus, das Gruseln zwischen Buchdeckeln zu lernen, den verdrängten Aberwitz alltäglicher Wirklichkeitserfahrung in fremder Phantasie auszuleben? Für Spannung jedenfalls ist gesorgt, thematisch wie formal: »His stories always have a nasty sting in the tail.« Die überraschende Schlußwendung, die Neigung zum Grotesken sind zu Warenzeichen von Dahls Erzählungen geworden. *Tales of the Unexpected* heißt folgerichtig der Titel der Neuausgabe von fünfundzwanzig seiner bekanntesten Geschichten zur gleichnamigen Fernsehserie. Die absolute Zuspitzung der Handlung auf die unerwartete Pointe nimmt freilich einigen Texten bei wiederholtem Lesen viel von ihrem ursprünglichen Reiz, und manche (u. a. »The Hitch-hiker«, »The Great Switcheroo«, »Vengeance is Mine Inc.«) sind kaum mehr als hochglanzpolierte »cock-and-bull stories«. Dahl ist sich dessen womöglich bewußt, wenn er feststellt: »I am primarily a short-story writer. But a good plot is hard to find, and it gets harder all the time. No short-story writer should continue when he has run out of plots.«[2] Seit *Kiss Kiss* (1959) ist Dahl selten fündig geworden. Seine Poetik ist von robuster Schlichtheit: »My job, if I write a story, is purely to entertain. If there is an undercurrent of social commentary running through it, this is not done purposefully. That's just how you feel, about people

1 Dies gilt auch für seine Kinderbücher. Nicht ohne Stolz bemerkt Dahl: »I suppose I could knock at the door of any house where there was a child – whether it was the US, Britain, Holland, West Germany, France – [. . .]. And they'd know me. That does make me feel good.« (Zit. nach: Chris Powling, *Roald Dahl*, Harmondsworth 1985, S. 78.)

2 Zit. nach: James Vinson (Hrsg.), *Contemporary Novelists*, London 1976, S. 317.

and things, and that's bound to creep into your writing occasionally.«[3] Über den Verdacht, ein angriffslustiger Satiriker oder bissiger Moralist zu sein, will er erhaben bleiben.

Und doch unterscheidet sich Dahl wohltuend von der uniformen Masse professioneller Gänsehautbeschwörer und Phantasten. Die schaurige Kulisse hat er nicht nötig, um eine beklemmende Atmosphäre zu erzeugen. Seine Erzählungen sind fast demonstrativ in der Alltagswelt angesiedelt, ihre Schauplätze wirken eher zufällig; die Figuren entstammen meist der Mittelschicht, Ehepaare und leichte Sonderlinge sind seine bevorzugten Protagonisten.[4] Um so drastischer allerdings die Wirkung, wenn sich in einem derartigen Allerweltsmilieu Befremdliches ereignet. Auch dabei geht Dahl eigene Wege. Anders als in der traditionellen »gothic tale« bricht das Böse oder Wunderbare nur selten von außen in die Welt der Figuren ein, sondern entsteht in ihrem Bewußtsein, um sich bedrohlich wie ein Flaschengeist plötzlich zu materialisieren:

> »He regarded it [the carpet] gravely [. . .]. He had never really noticed it before, but now all of a sudden, the colours seemed to brighten mysteriously and spring out at him in a most dazzling way. You see, he told himself, I know how it is. The red parts of the carpet are red-hot lumps of coal [. . .]. If I touch the red I will be burnt. As a matter of fact, I will be burnt up completely. And the black parts of the carpet . . . yes, the black parts are snakes, poisonous snakes [. . .], and if I touch one of *them*, I'll be bitten and I'll die« (S. 48).

Wenig später ist die Materialisierung vollzogen:

> »Another snake slid noiselessly beside the first, raised its head [. . .] gazing at a little naked place just below the sandal strap where the skin showed through. The child went high up on his toes and stayed there, frozen stiff with terror« (S. 51).

Der Wechsel von der Innen- zur Außenperspektive mit dem letzten Satz verstärkt den Eindruck eines realen Geschehens.

3 Zit. nach: Peter Firchow (Hrsg.), *The Writer's Place. Interviews on the Literary Situation in Contemporary Britain*, Minneapolis 1974, S. 100.

4 Der Titel *Someone Like You* – Dahl verwendet ihn bereits in *Over to You. 10 Stories of Flyers and Flying* (1946) – ist in dieser Hinsicht programmatisch.

Die sprachliche Ökonomie, welche die Short Story fordert, kommt Dahl entgegen. Einige wenige suggestive Einzelheiten genügen ihm, um Lebensumstände und Charakter seiner Figuren einprägsam darzustellen:

> »She glanced over at William's empty chair on the other side of the fireplace. It was a big brown leather armchair, and there was a depression on the seat of it, made by his buttocks over the years. Higher up, on the backrest, there was a dark oval stain on the leather where his head had rested« (S. 6).

Der Eindruck, den ihr Mann hinterlassen hat (nicht nur im übertragenen Sinn), ist stark genug, Mrs Pearl an ihre Pflicht zu erinnern: »Slowly she reached into her handbag and took out her spectacles and [. . .] started to read« (ebd.).

Scheinbar belanglose Nebensächlichkeiten – ein kleiner Junge löst ein Stückchen Schorf vom Knie ab – prägen sich dem Leser ein durch die Resonanz der bestätigenden Eigenerfahrung und vermitteln so mit dem intensiven Eindruck von Authentizität ein deutliches Identifikationsangebot. Dahl hat den Ratschlag, den ihm C. S. Forester, der Verfasser der populären Hornblower-Romane, gab, beherzigt: »[. . .] plenty of detail. That's what counts in our business, tiny little details, like you had a broken shoelace on your left shoe . . . or the man you were talking to had a broken fronttooth.«[5] Anders als sein Ratgeber aber setzt Dahl das Detail selten nur vordergründig ein, um Lokalkolorit zu erzeugen, sondern benutzt es als Mittel präziser Beschreibung und Sympathielenkung: »[. . .] the lower lip hanging downward in the centre, a pendulous, permanently open taster's lip, shaped open to receive the rim of a glass or a morsel of food. Like a keyhole, I thought, watching it; his mouth is like a large wet keyhole.«[6]

Ein weiteres wesentliches Kennzeichen von Dahls Kurzgeschichten ist die nüchtern-distanzierte Erzählhaltung. Sie hat Anlaß zu dem Mißverständnis gegeben, der Autor sei herzlos und grausam. Gerade aber die emotionale Enthaltsamkeit seiner Erzähler veranlaßt den Leser weit eher als eine einfühlende

5 »Lucky Break«, in: *The Wonderful Story of Henry Sugar and Six More*, Harmondsworth 1984, S. 214.

6 »Taste«, in: *Someone Like You*, Harmondsworth 1982, S. 17.

Darstellung dazu, das vorgestellte Verhalten kritisch zu beurteilen. Dahl vermeidet es gewissenhaft, vorfabrizierte Gefühlswerte zu vermitteln; Passagen der folgenden Art, wie sie etwa bei Poe gang und gäbe sind, wird man bei ihm vergeblich suchen:

»And now at the dead hour of the night, amid the dreadful silence of that old house, so strange a noise as this excited me to uncontrollable terror« (»The Tell-Tale Heart«).

». . . and a consciousness of the entire and terrible truth flashed suddenly over my soul« (»The Assignation«).

Dahls Erzähler übernehmen meist die Funktion von Zeugen; Zeugen, die im entscheidenden Augenblick schweigen und es dem Leser überlassen, »die Erkenntnis der ganzen entsetzlichen Wahrheit« wie einen Blitz durch seine Seele zucken zu lassen. Dies gilt selbst dann, wenn ein erlebendes Ich wie Lionel Lampton in »Nunc Dimittis« sich unmittelbar an den Leser wendet, für den – da er den Titel der Erzählung kennt – kein Zweifel daran bestehen kann, was die letzten Sätze, die Lampton zu Papier bringt, bedeuten:

»I haven't been feeling any too chipper this last hour or so. Perhaps I ought to go up right away and get myself some bicarbonate of soda. I can easily come back and finish this later, when I'm in better trim.

You know – now I come to think of it, I really do feel rather ill of a sudden.«[7]

Ein Rezensent des *Times Literary Supplement* hat diese Technik eindrucksvoll beschrieben:

»He thinks of a story as of a staircase up which the reader is to be lured and finally coaxed into taking that confident last step which, breathtakingly and deliciously, isn't there.«[8]

Um im Bild zu bleiben, es ist die Phantasie des Lesers, die ins Stolpern gerät, wenn die Handlung unerwartet abbricht. Die »große Szene« wird häufig sorgfältig angebahnt, nur um schließlich vorenthalten zu werden.

7 »Nunc Dimittis«, ebd., S. 189. Vgl. Lk 2,29: »Nunc dimittis servum tuum, Domine, secundum verbum tuum in pace.«

8 Vgl. Anon., »Roald Dahl, *Someone Like You*«, in: *Times Literary Supplement* 3083 (1961) S. 206.

Das Schreckliche, das Makabre vollzieht sich bei Dahl meist im Bewußtsein des Lesenden, nur selten wie in »Pig« im Text. Dazu gehört die schockartige Erkenntnis der wahren Zusammenhänge, verbunden mit dem Gefühl, eben diese Zusammenhänge längst geahnt zu haben. Ein Gefühl, das kaum trügt, weil Dahl den Weg zur Pointe mit Andeutungen markiert, die im Rückblick Stimmigkeit erzeugen. So in »Pig«, wo der tumbe Held auf die Frage, ob der deliziöse Braten, der ihm vorgesetzt wurde, wirklich vom Schwein war, zur Antwort erhält: »There's just a chance, you see, that it might have been a piece of human stuff. [. . .] As a matter of fact, we've been getting an awful lot of it just lately from the butcher's in place of pork« (S. 81). Der Leser mag zu diesem Zeitpunkt noch unsicher sein, ob der Koch sich nur einen Scherz mit Lexington erlaubt, sollte später jedoch nicht allzu überrascht sein, wenn der vegetarische Parsifal sein Ende im Schlachthaus nimmt, wo eine seiner letzten Wahrnehmungen ein Schwein mit langen weißen Handschuhen ist. Die Logik des Absurden in diesem Antimärchen vom »American Dream« bringt es mit sich, daß mit dem Helden noch andere Opfer im »Visitors' Waiting-Room« der Fleischfabrik sitzen: »And there was a pale woman with long white gloves, who sat very upright, with her hands folded on her lap« (S. 83). Es ist die ungerührte Selbstverständlichkeit, mit der solche Geschehnisse vermittelt werden, auf der die halluzinatorische Leseerfahrung bei Dahl beruht.

Als literarische Vorbilder für diese Art Erzählung kommen Ambrose Bierce (1842–1914?), Saki (1870–1916) und vor allem John Collier (1901–80) in Betracht. Bereits in Dahls Fliegergeschichten, *Over to You*, die sich im übrigen noch stark an Hemingway orientieren, scheint sich der Einfluß dieser Meister des Danse macabre zu zeigen. So tut der Leser am Ende von »Death of an Old Old Man« auf den Spuren von Bierce den Schritt ins Leere,[9] und in »An African Story« findet sich zum ersten Mal bei Dahl das für ihn wie Collier gleichermaßen unentbehrliche Rache-Motiv. Colliers Kurzgeschichtensamm-

9 Vgl. den Schluß von »Death of an Old Old Man« mit dem von Bierces »An Occurrence at Owl Creek Bridge«.

lung *Presenting Moonshine* (1941) läßt über thematische Anklänge hinaus eine deutliche Seelenverwandtschaft der beiden Autoren erkennen.[10] Dazu gehört neben der notorischen »stiff upper lip« ihrer Erzähler eine Grundhaltung, die Dahl einmal so umschrieben hat:

> »The best way of learning about people is first of all to learn about their foibles and filthy habits; then you can blackmail them on paper. People have far less nice characteristics than nasty ones, all people, and they all pretend to have far less nasty than nice ones.«[11]

Eine Erfahrung, die er, wie *Boy. Tales of Childhood* und die autobiographische Skizze »Lucky Break« zeigen, früh machen mußte, und die trotz der offensichtlichen Komik seiner Erzählungen für eine Grundstimmung sorgt, die nicht von ungefähr an Voltaires *Candide* erinnert.

Radikale Skepsis zeigt der Roman *Some Time Never* aus dem Jahr 1948, in dem Phantasiewesen, die Gremlins, (mit Erfolg) auf die Selbstvernichtung des Menschen warten, um die Erde selbst in Besitz zu nehmen. Der erste Teil schildert auf seine Art die »Battle of Britain«[12] (hier lehnt sich Dahl stark an seine ersten Geschichten an), der zweite eine apokalyptische Zukunft nach dem Zweiten Weltkrieg. Wenn auch formal und in manch anderer Hinsicht nicht ganz geglückt, verdient dieses in Vergessenheit geratene Werk weit eher Aufmerksamkeit als eine Albernheit wie *My Uncle Oswald*, zeigt es doch einen wenig bekannten Dahl, jenen Satiriker und Moralisten nämlich, der er später – nach der reservierten Aufnahme des Romans? – nicht mehr sein wollte. Zur Illustration ein Ausschnitt aus einer Rede, die der Anführer der Gremlins an sein Volk hält:

> »›Who is the human creature?‹ he shrieked. ›Who is he? [. . .] He is a hairless, two-legged black- or whiteskinned animal who crawls about upon his tiny earth with a wrinkled brow and a doubting face, understanding nothing, seeing nothing,

10 Vgl. Colliers »Green Thoughts«, »Mary« und »Squirrels Have Bright Eyes« mit Dahls »The Sound Machine«, »Pig« und »The Landlady«.

11 Zit. nach: Firchow, S. 100.

12 Bezeichnung für die Luftschlacht zwischen August und Oktober 1940, die die Invasion Englands vorbereiten sollte.

absorbed completely in his plans for improving his own personal lot. For a handful of years, for the brief tick of time in which he lives, he proceeds with a fierce and fervid concentration about the business which concerns himself. He does not pause to think how small he is, to think that in a moment he'll be gone, leaving behind him nothing but a heap of bones and the faint savour of his selfishness. He does not pause to wonder at the length of time which has no length, the size of space which has no size, the numbers of other larger worlds around him which are numberless; rather does he hope complacently to conquer time and space and other worlds by some strange miracle, which, when he is dead, will make him last forever. He laughs at the spider, at the ant and at the beetle, thinking that they are small, that he is great, forgetting that in proportion to the sizeless size of space, there's no more difference between a beetle and a man than there might be between two grains of sand.‹«[13]

Dahl ist (wie Bierce) geprägt vom Alptraumerlebnis des Krieges, dessen barbarische Absurdität eine rationale Bewältigung unmöglich macht. Wo menschliche Vernunft die Segel streicht, übernehmen Gremlins das Ruder. Das Trauma, das in *Over to You* und *Some Time Never* zutage tritt, findet im makabren und grotesken Geschehen der späteren Kurzgeschichten seine Fortsetzung. Recht besehen erweisen sich *Someone Like You* und *Kiss Kiss* als Anthologien menschlicher Destruktivität:

»Phantastik [. . .] beschwört [. . .] nicht ein namenloses und unfaßbares Unheil, sondern benennt [. . .] die verschwiegenen und verborgenen Gefährdungen des Menschen durch die von Menschen gemachte und zu verantwortende Welt. Phantastik ist die Wiederkehr des Verdrängten.«[14]

Roald Dahl kann uns daran erinnern.

Harald Beck

13 *Some Time Never*, New York 1948, S. 113.

14 Joachim Metzner, »Die Vieldeutigkeit der Wiederkehr. Literaturpsychologische Überlegungen zur Phantastik«, in: Christian W. Thomsen / Jens Malte Fischer (Hrsg.), *Phantastik in Literatur und Kunst*, Darmstadt 1980, S. 108.